THE BARBER
OF SEVILLE

PIERRE-AUGUSTIN CARON DE
BEAUMARCHAIS

The Barber
of Seville

or
THE USELESS PRECAUTION

TRANSLATED AND EDITED BY

Brobury Pearce Ellis

CENTRAL CONNECTICUT STATE COLLEGE

New York

APPLETON-CENTURY-CROFTS

Division of Meredith Publishing Company

INTRODUCTION

Both *The Barber of Seville* and its sequel, *The Marriage of Figaro,* have been tremendously popular for a very long time, although, to be sure, they are better known in this country as Italian operas than as French comedies. Even in disguise, Beaumarchais' delightful characters continue to shine—above all, the *veritable Figaro.* Eugene Lintilhac declared that the famous name now shared by a street and a newspaper in Paris was derived from the words *fils Caron,* thereby asserting the identity of character and author. The enormous vitality of Beaumarchais-Figaro keeps these plays alive, and we should know them better in our own language. As he himself said, wit loses some of its sparkle for people who don't understand the words.

Both comedies were popular from the beginning. *The Barber of Seville* was as successful as any play of its time; during its first year in the repertoire of the Comédie-Française it was performed twenty-seven times before some twenty-four thousand people. *The Marriage of Figaro* was by far the greatest hit of the century; during its first year it was performed seventy-three times before some ninety-seven thousand spectators. We have here something more than clever theatrical entertainment. Figaro's vitality includes more than his power to provoke laughter; he is one of the great symbols in the continuing fight for human freedom that links our time with his.

The brilliant author of these masterpieces was not primarily a writer at all. In one of his letters he said, "After the necessary business of one's affairs, everyone has his own favorite amusement: he hunts, or drinks, or gambles; but I, having none of these tastes, toss off plays for the theater." He had no standing in purely literary circles. One of his many contributions to human welfare was his organization of the Société des Auteurs Dramatiques in 1777, to protect writers in their dealings with actors. But he had to accomplish this almost in spite of the dramatists it was intended to help, all of whom distrusted him, because of his versatility, even more than they distrusted each other.

Beaumarchais little resembled the specialists who are our successful men today. He turned his hand to a great many diverse activities during his lifetime, which coincided exactly with that of George Washington. He was born the son of a watchmaker named Caron. Before he was twenty he invented a new escapement of such value that it was stolen from him, thus precipitating his first experience at standing up for his rights —the beginning of a life of litigation.

It was the beginning of his early success as well. While regaining credit for his invention he won favorable attention at the court of Louis XV. His subsequent invention of a new pedal arrangement for the harp led to an intimate acquaintance with the King's four daughters, whom he visited frequently at Versailles. This friendship in turn enabled him to do a service for one of France's most powerful financiers, Joseph Pâris-Duverney, who took a liking to him, giving him help and advice that soon made him a wealthy business man.

From then on Beaumarchais' life was a succession of spectacular falls and rises, both in business and at court. He had a hand in everything and he met everybody. An amazing adventure in Madrid, where he went to help a sister in trouble, included a personal interview with King Charles III and provided the story of Goethe's play *Clavigo*. He returned from another fantastic escapade with a large diamond ring, personally presented to him by the Empress Maria Theresa in Vienna. Every reader of the plays should turn to Georges Lemaitre's fascinating biography, both because of the intrinsic interest of Beaumarchais' exciting life and because of the light the events of his life throw upon the plays and the characters.

Beaumarchais' career as an author began with a few sketches he wrote for the private theater of Charles Lenormant at Etioles, where in 1766 *The Barber of Seville* first appeared. After writing two unsuccessful plays in the sentimental vein of bourgeois drama, *Eugénie* in 1767 and *The Two Friends* in 1770, he rewrote his sketch about the Spanish barber in 1771 for the Italian comedians in Paris. Since the Italians had merged with the Opéra-Comique, he wrote it as a comic opera, composing and arranging the music himself.

The Italians should have felt at home in it, for the plot, the characters, and even some of the situations are directly borrowed from the Italian comic tradition which runs all the way back to ancient Greece and had long been a familiar influence throughout Europe. The story of a young lover who, with the help of a confidant, wins his lady out from under the nose of a jealous old man was just about the oldest of all; in one of its variations it served as the subplot of Shakespeare's *The Taming of the Shrew*. And Beaumarchais' old doctor even bears a traditional name: Doctor Baloardo (a word meaning gross and stupid) first appeared in Bologna about the year 1500, a variation on a still more ancient character designed to ridicule the pedants at the university. Furthermore, the author slyly calls attention to the timeworn aspect of one of his situations: "These stories of substitute teachers are old tricks in all the comedies," as we know, since that too appears in *The Taming of the Shrew*.

And yet the Italians rejected his work, for a reason the author could hardly have foreseen: a leading actor who had once worked as a barber felt embarrassed at the thought of appearing in a play about one. Undismayed, Beaumarchais rewrote it again as a four-act comedy, and in this form the Comédie-Française scheduled it for performance in 1773. At the last minute it was cancelled because the author was involved in a particularly notorious scandal. When it was rescheduled the following year, Beaumarchais revised it again, adding a fifth act and spreading a tone of bitterness throughout the play that darkened its comic aspect considerably.

Although these changes were disastrous, Beaumarchais had good reason for the strong feelings he thus betrayed. He was struggling unsuccessfully for justice against the Comte de la Blache in courts that repeatedly upheld his noble adversary, even though right was clearly on his side. His only weapon was an appeal to public opinion by means of a series of published bulletins, called *Mémoires*. In the fourth of these he denounced a venial judge named Goëzman, who refused to return a bribe of fifteen louis after deciding a point against him. Jules Janin described its overwhelming significance:

In this cause, and on account of fifteen louis, Beaumarchais set a clear course for the rhetoricians who were later to overthrow the old France, which seemed still to be in good health but was actually riddled with decay. It was a great discovery this man made on the day when he first expressed the idea that came to dominate the period. Beaumarchais found his proper title in a society that no longer knew why it was concerned with Beaumarchais.

'I am a citizen,' Beaumarchais cried, 'I am a citizen! That is to say, I am neither a courtier, nor a churchman, nor a gentleman, nor a businessman, nor a favorite, nor anything that is regarded as powerful nowadays. I am a citizen! That is to say, something altogether new, something unknown, unprecedented in France. I am a citizen! That is to say, what you should have been for the past two hundred years, what you will be perhaps in twenty years.'

At this name, so new in 1774, society remained attentive and silent. Beaumarchais was known to be playing a game that had never before been played by anyone. The France of that time clearly recalled that it had seen princes of the blood raising a standard of revolt, parliaments opposing the King's justice, Jesuits putting the state to fire and sword on account of papal bulls; but what France had not seen was a man alone, a common man accused by a crowd, a poor devil without ancestors, without supporters, without protection, less than nothing, lifting his head suddenly, becoming all at once taller than the height of Parliament, speaking to her face to face and out loud, as equal to equal, if not as her master.

No, France had never seen such a rebellion. And, as she is a noble country that respects every kind of courage, she applauded the courage of this earthworm who did not wish to be squashed by Judge Goëzman.

In this mood Beaumarchais revised his merry comedy before its first performance. The frail structure of traditional comedy can contain only so much emotion as strong as that of the fourth *Mémoire*. Thus, in its first performance in February, 1775, the play was virtually swamped, a fact that the author made much of in his preface. Nevertheless, Beaumarchais was quick to see what was wrong. Before the second performance, he cut it to four acts again and toned down the bitterest of his gibes; from then on its success was unbroken.

Beaumarchais began work on *The Marriage of Figaro* before the end of the same year. As he said, it began with a suggestion from his friend, the Prince de Conti, that he use the imaginary "sixth act" sketched in his preface to *The Barber of Seville*. But during the nine years before the sequel was first performed in public, Figaro matured, becoming something vastly greater than the confidant of traditional comedy. I hope that every reader of this play will read the other as well, to see for himself what a fine fellow Figaro ultimately turned out to be.

B. P. E.

PRINCIPAL DATES
IN THE LIFE OF BEAUMARCHAIS

❧

1732   Birth of Pierre-Augustin Caron on January 24.

1753   As a watchmaker working with his father, invented an escapement mechanism still in use today.

1756   Married a widow named Franquet and took the name of Beaumarchais from a small property of hers.

1763   Became a judge with jurisdiction over game laws.

1764   Travelled to Spain to help his sister Lisette with her fiancé, Clavijo, a Spanish journalist.

1767   *Eugénie* performed.

1770   *The Two Friends,* or *The Merchant of Lyons* performed.

1775   *The Barber of Seville,* or, *The Useless Precaution* performed.

1776   Formed Roderigue Hortalez & Co. to provide supplies for the American Revolution, a few weeks before the signing of the Declaration of Independence.

1778   Formed the *Société typographique et littéraire* for the publication of the complete works of Voltaire.

1784   *A Mad Day's Work*, or, *The Marriage of Figaro* performed.

1787   *Tarare*, a philosophical opera, performed.

1792   *The Guilty Mother* performed.

1799   Death of Beaumarchais on May 18.

TEMPERATE LETTER

about the failure and the condemnation of

THE BARBER OF SEVILLE

(Modestly dressed and bowing low, the author presents his play to the reader.)

Sir,

I have the honor to offer you a new little work of mine. I hope to meet you in one of those rare moments—free from care, content with your health, with your business, with your mistress, with your dinner, with your stomach— when you are in a mood to amuse yourself for a little while by reading my *Barber of Seville*. All these conditions are required before you are a man capable of amusement and an indulgent reader.

But if any accident has disturbed your health, if your affairs are in a critical state, if your loved one broke her promises, if your dinner was bad, or your digestion is upset—then put down my *Barber*. This is no time for it. Go over your budget; study the *factum* issued by your enemy; read over the treacherous letter to Rose that you intercepted; or go through Tissot's masterpieces on temperance and spin theories about politics, economics, dietetics, philosophy, or morality.

Or, if your condition is such that forgetfulness eludes you altogether, sink into an armchair and open the paper published in Bouillon with encyclopedia, consent, and privilege,[1] and quickly drop off to sleep for an hour or two.

What charm has a merry play when you have the black vapors? And what is it to you, for that matter, if Figaro the barber befools Bartholo the doctor by helping a rival to spirit away his sweetheart from him? It's hard to enter into the merriment of others when you're out of sorts yourself.

Furthermore, what is it to you if this Spanish barber, upon his arrival in Paris, endures certain misfortunes, and if the banning of his performance confers undue importance upon the bees buzzing in my bonnet? One can hardly concern himself with the affairs of others when he's uncertain about his own.

But you're sure that all is well with you? Have you all you could wish for in a strong stomach, a good cook, a faithful mistress, and sound sleep? Then let's sit down and give my *Barber* a hearing.

I feel strongly, sir, that it's no longer the time to hold back my manuscript, like a coquette who often denies what she's always dying to give, granting only miserly private readings of it to privileged people who feel bound to repay my courtesy with pompous eulogies upon my work.

Those were happy days! The place, the time, the audience were all devoted to me. With the magic of a clever reading to assure my success, I skipped lightly over the weak little play, emphasizing the good passages. Then, when I observed their approval out of the corner of my eye with modest pride, I revelled in a triumph that was all

---

[1] *The Encyclopedic Journal by a Society of Literary Men* was known as a "peripheral" magazine because it was published outside the capital city of Paris. Nevertheless, it was highly influential, and Beaumarchais took great pains to answer all the objections to his play that appeared in it, while denigrating the talents of its writers. Consent and privilege refer to the license from the King required on publications of all kinds.

the sweeter because no performance by a rascally actor had stolen three quarters of it from me for his own account.

But here I have none of that bag of tricks. At a time when it would take miracles to impress you, when Moses' wand would hardly suffice, I have scarcely the power of Jacob's staff. No juggling, no trickery, no coquetry, no vocal inflections, no theatrical illusion—nothing. You will judge my virtues unadorned.

You must not think it strange, sir, if, suiting my style to my situation, I do not do as those writers do who put on a casual air by addressing you as *reader, friend reader, dear reader, benign* or *indulgent reader,* or any of those other high-handed—I might even say indecent—appellations by means of which imprudent writers try to put themselves on a par with their judge, and which often succeed only in drawing adverse criticism. I have always noticed that superficial manners deceive no one; only a modest tone in an author wins a little indulgence from his fine reader.

Ah! what writer ever had more need of it than I! It would be useless to deny it. At different times I was foolish enough to present you with two pathetic dramas, monstrosities, as everyone knows. For now we know that nothing at all exists between tragedy and comedy. The point is settled. The master has enunciated it, and the school resounds with it. As for me, I'm so thoroughly convinced of it that if I wanted to put on the stage a distressed mother, a betrayed wife, a distracted sister, or a disinherited son, I would begin, in order to present them properly to the public, by inventing for them some beautiful kingdom where they rule wisely, off in one of the archipelagos, or some other corner of the earth. After that, I could be quite confident that the improbability of the story, its exaggerated situations, bombastic characters, outlandish ideas, and inflated language, far from being regarded as faults, would even ensure my success.

Portray ordinary men in difficulty and unhappiness? Never! They must only be scoffed at. Ridiculous common people and unhappy kings: there is all the theater that exists and all that is possible. I take it to be settled. It's done, and I have no wish to quarrel any more with anyone.

So I was misguided formerly, sir, when I wrote dramas that weren't "the right kind." I deeply repent.

Under the pressure of circumstances, I later undertook my ill-fated *Mémoires,* which my enemies found to be not in "the right style." I suffer cruelly from remorse.

Today I insinuate before your eyes an exceedingly gay comedy that certain arbiters of taste consider not to have "the right tone." I am inconsolable.

Perhaps some day I will dare to assault your ears with an opera, and the young men of those times will say that the music is not written in "good French." For that I am abashed in advance.

And so, between asking pardon for my faults, and making excuses for my mistakes, I will spend my life to earn your forgiveness, by the simple good faith with which I acknowledge the former and offer you the latter.

As for *The Barber of Seville,* I'm not taking a respectful tone here in an attempt to influence your judgment of it. But I have been positively assured that when an author emerges victorious from the theater, however battered he might be, he needs only to be approved by you, sir, and to be flayed in certain journals, to have won all the literary laurels. Then my glory is assured if you deign to grant me the laurel of your approval, for I am sure that many gentlemen of the press will not refuse me the laurel of their disparagement.

Already one of them, set up in Bouillon "with consent and privilege," has done me the "encyclopedic" honor to assure his subscribers that my play has no plan, no unity, no characters, is devoid of plot and bare of comedy.

Another, even more naive, to be sure without "consent," without "privilege," and even without "encyclopedia," after candidly exposing my drama, added to the laurel of his condemnation this flattering eulogy of my person: "Mr Beaumarchais' reputation is altogether deflated. Decent people are finally convinced that when his peacock feathers are snatched away, nothing more will remain than an evil black raven, with all his presumption and his voracity."

Since I have had, so to speak, the presumption to write the comedy of *The Barber of Seville,* in order to fulfill the rest of the horoscope, I will push the voracity so far as humbly to beg you, sir, to judge me yourself, without regard to critics past, present, and future; for you know that by profession journalists are often the enemies of literary men. I will even be voracious enough to inform you beforehand that, having taken up my work, you must be the absolute judge, whether you want to or not, because you are my reader.

And you are surely aware, sir, that if you continually refuse to read me, either to avoid this annoyance, or to prove to me that I reason falsely, you will be begging the question, according to your lights; not being my reader, you are not the man to whom my request is directed.

What if you decide to throw down the book at this point in your reading because you are irritated by the burden I propose to place on you? Then, sir, it is as if, in the middle of quite another judgment, you were removed from the bench by death, or some accident that expunged you from the number of magistrates. You may avoid judging me only by becoming null, void, and nonexistent, only by ceasing to exist in the character of my reader.

Well, what harm do I do you by placing you above me? Next to the pleasure of commanding men, isn't the greatest honor, sir, to judge them?

There, it's all arranged. I recognize no other judge but you, not excepting the audiences who, since they have only a first impression to go on, often find their verdict set aside by your tribunal.

The case was argued first before them in the theater. Since they laughed a great deal, I was led to think that I had won my case with the audience. Not at all; the journalist set up in Bouillon maintains that they laughed at *me*. But there's nothing in that contention, sir, as they say in the courts, but a lawyer's poor quibble. Since my aim was to amuse the audience, it doesn't matter whether they laughed at my play or at me; so long as they laughed heartily, my aim was fulfilled as well one way as the other. I call that winning my case with the audience.

The same journalist assures us further, or at least leads us to understand, that I sought to win over certain gentlemen, buying their approval in advance, by giving them private readings of the play. But there's nothing in that, sir, but the objection of a German political writer. It is manifest that my intention was only to instruct them; it was a kind of consultation that I carried on concerning the basis of the case. What if the consultants, after giving their advice, mingled with the judges? You can certainly see, sir, that I could do nothing about it. It was for them to disqualify themselves out of delicacy, if they felt any partiality toward my Andalusian barber.

Ah, would to heaven they might have kept a little for this young foreigner! We would have had a little less trouble in defending our unhappy dayfly. Men are like that. When you're successful they honor you, support you, flatter you, they glory in you; but beware of stumbling along the course. At the least check, O my friends! bear in mind that he's no longer a friend.

And that's just what happened to us on the morning after the saddest of evenings. You would have seen the weak friends of *The Barber* scatter, hide their faces, or cover themselves with earth; the women, always so brave when they defend us, plunge into their hoods, feathers and all, and lower their eyes in confusion; the men running to visit each other to make honorable amends for the good that they have spoken about my play, and blaming all the false pleasure they had tasted in it on my wretched style of reading it. It was a total desertion, a true desolation.

Some gazed off to the left when they felt me passing on the right, no longer seeming to see me. Ye gods! Some were more courageous, but, making sure they were unobserved, they drew me into a corner before telling me, "Well, how did you manage to fool us like that? You must admit, my friend, that your play is the greatest platitude in the world."

"Alas, sirs, I read my platitude, to tell the truth, just as flatly as I wrote it. But for the sake of the kindness that you have to speak to me again after my defeat, and for the honor of your second judgment, never let the play be revived in the theater; if by some mischance the play should be performed then as I read it, you may have a new deception played on you, and you will blame me for not knowing when you're right and when you're wrong, God forbid."

They didn't believe me. The play was revived, and, as it turned out, I was a prophet in my own country. Poor Figaro, spanked by the claque in plainsong and almost buried on Friday, was not like Candide. He roused his courage, and my poor hero rose up again on Sunday with a vigor that the austerity of an entire Lent and the wear of seventeen public performances has not yet diminished. But who knows how long this will last? I wouldn't be willing to swear that the point won't arise for another five or six centuries, because our people are so fickle and frivolous!

The works of the theater, sir, are like the children born of woman. Conceived with pleasure, carried for their term with fatigue, brought forth in pain, and rarely living to repay their parents for their care, they cause more trouble than they yield pleasure. Follow them in their careers: hardly have they seen the light of day than, under pretense of bombast, censors are applied to them; many remain in prison. Instead of playing happily with them, the audience bullies them and makes them fail. Often, while nursing them, the actors cripple them. If you lose sight of them for a moment, you will find them, alas! spread out everywhere, but tattered, disfigured, with pieces gnawed away, and covered with criticisms. If they survive all these perils and shine for a moment in public, the greatest evil of all awaits them: mortal forgetfulness kills them. They die, plunge again into nothingness, and are lost forever in the huge mass of books.

I asked someone the reason for these battles, this lively warfare between the audience and the author at the first performance of a new play, even of those that turn out later to be successful. "Don't you know," he replied, "that Sophocles and Dionysius the Elder died of joy when they won prizes for their plays? [2] We love our authors too much to allow an excess of joy to deprive us of them by suffocating them. In order to preserve them we take pains to see that their triumph is never so complete that they might die of the pleasure of it."

Whatever the motive of this severity, the child of my spare time, this young and innocent *Barber,* so greatly scorned at first, on the second day after his triumph has no disposition to abuse his critics or to imitate their bad

---

[2] When Beaumarchais is having fun, he allows himself certain liberties with fact. The story about Sophocles, the great tragedian of Athens, is one among several unsubstantiated traditions of his death in the year 406 B.C. Dionysius the Elder, tyrant of Syracuse, was a military man who aspired, with little success, to fame as a tragedian. Hence, when he heard that his tragedy *The Ransom of Hector* had received first prize in the year 367 B.C., his joy was great enough to overcome his disappointment in a recent military setback. In celebration, he drank so much wine that he fell into a fever and never awoke after a soporific drink was administered to him as a cure.

humor; he is only the more eager to disarm them by the playfulness of his character.

This is a rare and striking example, sir, in an age of cavilling, where everything is calculated, including laughter; where the slightest divergence of opinion germinates eternal hate; where all games turn into war; where the injury done to repair another is in its turn repaid with a third, until each one, while effacing the last, breeds many others, thus propagating bitterness into infinity, until laughter gives way to satiety and disgust, to the indignation of even the most caustic reader.

As for me, sir, if it is true, as they say, that all men are brothers (and it is a beautiful idea), I wish it were possible to persuade our brothers the literary men to abandon the haughty and cutting tone they employ in debate with our brothers the libellists, who do their work so well! as well as the insults to our brothers the litigants . . . who do theirs no worse! Most of all, I wish that our brothers the journalists could be persuaded to renounce the pedagogical and magisterial tone with which they thump Apollo's son, and cause stupidity to laugh at the expense of intelligence.

Open a paper: don't you seem to see a harsh tutor with a ferrule or a rod raised over the dilatory pupils, treating them like slaves at the slightest neglect of duty? Ah, my brothers, much this has to do with duty! Literature is release from it, a pleasant recreation.

As for me at least, in this game don't try to pin down my wit to the rules; it is incorrigible. Once the schoolroom of duty is closed, it becomes so light and waggish that I can do nothing but play with it. Like a feathered cork that bounces on the racket, it soars, it falls again, it delights my eyes, sets off again into the air, wheels, and returns again. If any clever player wishes to take part in this game and to bandy between us the light shuttlecock of my thoughts, he's heartily welcome; if he returns it with grace and facility the game delights me, and competition begins. Then you'll see volleys sustained, parried, received, returned, accelerated, pressed, picked up with such speed and clean agility as to make the spectators cheer on the players.

At least, sir, that is what the critic should be; and it is thus that I have always conceived disputes between polite people who cultivate literature.

Let's see, if you please, whether the journalist of Bouillon preserves in his criticism this characteristic of amiability, and above all of candor, that has just been prayed for.

He says, "The play is a farce."

Let's judge qualities. The horrid name that a foreign cook gives to French ragouts has no effect on their flavor. It's what he does to them that destroys their quality. Let's analyze the Bouillon farce.

"The play," he says, "has no form."

Is it because it's too simple that it escapes the sagacity of the adolescent critic?

An amorous old man intends to marry his ward the next day. A young lover, more adroit, gets ahead of him, and this same day makes her his wife under the eyes and in the house of her guardian. There's the basis of the play, of which you might make, with equal success, a tragedy, a comedy, a drama, an opera, etc. Is *The Miser* of Molière anything else? Is the great *Mithridates* anything else? The nature of a play, like that of any other deed, depends less on the basic acts themselves than it does on the characters who perform them.

As for me, since I wished to make no more of this situation than an amusing play that wouldn't tire anyone, a sort of imbroglio, it suited my purpose to have the man who sets it in motion not a black villain, but a droll boy, an imperturbable man, who laughs as much at the success as at the failure of his schemes; thus the work becomes no serious drama, but a very gay comedy. Because the guardian is a little less stupid than most characters who are duped on the stage, there is a great deal of action in the play, and, most of all, the necessity for a high degree of ingenuity in the plotters.

If I were not content with comic simplicity, if I had wished to complicate, expand, or twist my plot into tragedy or drama, can it be imagined that I would have been at a loss with this story, of which I put on the stage only the least wonderful part?

You see, everybody knows that at the time when the play ends merrily in my hands, the quarrel between Figaro and the doctor over the hundred ecus begins to grow seriously warm backstage, as it were. Insults lead to blows. Figaro thrashes the doctor; as he falls, he catches the net or fillet that holds the barber's hair, and there he discovers, to his surprise, the shape of a spatula branded on his shaved head. Follow me, sir, I beg you.

At the sight of this mark, soundly beaten as he is, the doctor cries with transports of joy, "My son, O heavens, my son, my dear son!" Before Figaro hears this, he redoubles his whacks on his dear father. In truth, that's who he was.

Figaro, who had previously known no family at all except his mother, is Bartholo's illegitimate son. The doctor in his youth got this child by a woman in service, the consequences of whose imprudence caused her to lose her position and move into the most frightful destitution.

But before leaving them, the desolate Bartholo, a village barber then, heated his spatula and branded his son on the occiput so that he might recognize him some day, if Fate ever reunited them. Mother and child passed six years in honorable beggary before a gypsy chief, crossing Andalusia with his band, whom the mother consulted about the destiny of her child, stole the child secretly and left this written horoscope in his place:

After shedding the blood from which he was born,
Your child will trounce his father forlorn;
Then, turning on himself the weapon and the crime,
He strikes himself and finds joy sublime.

When he changed his estate without knowing it, the poor young man also changed his name without wishing to. He was raised under the name of Figaro, and he survived. His mother is that Marceline, now the doctor's old housekeeper, who was consoled for her loss by the frightful horoscope. But today, all is fulfilled.

By bleeding Marceline's foot, as you see in my play, or rather as you do not see there, Figaro fulfills the first line: *After shedding the blood from which he was born.*

When he innocently thrashes the doctor, after the curtain falls, he carries out the second line: *Your child will trounce his father forlorn.*

At once the most touching recognition takes place between the doctor, the old lady, and Figaro: "It's you! it's he! it's you! it's I!" What a scene! But the son, overcome with remorse because of his innocent violence, melts in tears and gives himself a slash with the razor, according to the sense of the third line: *Then, turning on himself the weapon and the crime,/ He strikes himself . . .*

What a tableau! By not explaining whether Figaro cuts his throat or merely his beard, you see, I had a choice of finishing my play with the greatest pathos. At last, the doctor marries the old lady, and Figaro, following the last line: . . . *finds joy sublime.*

What an outcome! It would only have cost me a sixth act. And what a sixth act! Never a tragedy at the Théâtre-Français . . . enough said. Let's go back to my play as it was performed and criticized. When I'm bitterly attacked for what I've done, it's no time to praise what I could have done.

"The play lacks verisimilitude in its action," the journalist went on, who is established in Bouillon "with consent and privilege."

No verisimilitude! Let's examine that, just for the fun of it.

His Excellency the Count Almaviva, whose particular friend I have had the honor to be for some time, is a young nobleman, or more accurately was, for age and heavy responsibilities have since turned him into a very sober man, just as I myself have become. His Excellency was then a young Spanish nobleman, lively and ardent as any lover in his country. They are thought to be cold, but they are only lazy.

He set out secretly in pursuit of a beautiful maiden he had caught a glimpse of in Madrid and whose guardian immediately brought back to her birthplace. One morning, while walking under her windows in Seville, where he had been trying to get her to notice him since eight o'clock, chance brought to that same spot Figaro, the barber. "Ah! chance!" my critic will say: "And if chance had not brought the barber that day to that spot, what would become of the play?" "Brother, it would have begun some other day." "Impossible, since her guardian, in your own words, intends to marry her the next day." "Then there would have been no play, or, if there were, brother, it would have been different. Is a thing lacking in verisimilitude because it is possible that it could happen otherwise?"

Indeed, you're a little out of sorts. After all, the Cardinal of Retz tells us in cold blood, "One day I needed a man; to tell the truth, I only wanted a ghost. I would have liked him to be the grandson of Henry the Great, to have long blonde hair, to be beautiful, well-built, somewhat rebellious, to have the language and the love of the common people. And chance caused me to meet in Paris M. de Beaufort, escaped from the King's prison. He was exactly the man that I needed." Should we reply to the coadjutor,

"Ah, chance! What if you had not met M. de Beaufort?"
What if this? What if that?

So, chance led Figaro the barber to this same spot. He's
a good talker, a bad poet, a fearless musician, a great
strummer on the guitar, and at one time a valet to the
Count, now living in Seville, where he works successfully
on beards, romances, and marriages; plying with equal skill
the lancet of the phlebotomist and the syringe of the phar-
macist, the terror of husbands, the bird of wives, and exactly the man we need. Since in all courtship what we call
passion is only desire enflamed by frustration, the young
lover, who might have suffered only a passing inclination
for this beauty if he had met her in public, becomes enamored of her because she is locked up, in order to make
it impossible for him to marry her.

But to give you a complete summary of the play here,
sir, would be to doubt the sagacity and the quickness with
which you will take in the author's scheme and follow the
thread of the plot through a simple labyrinth. Since you
are less prejudiced than the journalist of Bouillon, who is
mistaken, "with consent and privilege," about all the action of the play, you will perceive that *all the pains of the
lover are* not *expended simply to deliver a letter,* which is
merely a minor part of the plot, but to take his position
in a fort defended by vigilance and suspicion; most of all,
to deceive a man who repeatedly sees through a maneuver,
forcing his enemy to reverse himself quickly to avoid being unhorsed at the first onset.

And when you see the fun at the climax arising from
the fact that the guardian locked his door and gave a pass-
key to Bazile, to make sure that only he and the notary
might enter to celebrate the wedding, you will never re-
cover from your astonishment that a reasonably just critic
trifles so far with his reader's confidence, or is mistaken
enough, to write, and in Bouillon at that, "Figaro and the
Count go to the trouble of climbing to the balcony on a
ladder, even though the door is unlocked."

Finally, when you see the unfortunate guardian, gulled by means of the very precautions he took to avoid being so, forced at the last to sign the Count's contract and to approve what he was unable to prevent, you will leave the critic to decide if the guardian was an *imbecile* not to see through the plot that was altogether hidden from him, whereas the critic, from whom nothing was hidden, was unable to see any more than the guardian.

For if he had been able to grasp it clearly, would he have failed to praise all the beautiful passages in the work?

He may be pardoned for not noticing the way in which all the characters in the play are introduced and shown in lively action in the very first act.

I can also easily conceive how he overlooked some little comedy in the big scene of the second act, where, in spite of mistrust and the fury of jealousy, the ward succeeds in fooling her guardian about a letter delivered in his presence, and to make him ask pardon on his knees for having suspected her.

I'm not at all surprised that he said not a single word about Bazile's scene of stupefaction in the third act, which stood out as something really new on the stage and utterly delighted the audience.

Let it pass too that he failed to observe the difficulty the author voluntarily put himself into in the last act when he allowed the ward to reveal to her guardian that the Count had stolen the key to the shutter, and how the author gets himself out of it in two words, and, in sheer sport, escapes from a new distress into which he had plunged the audience. It's a little thing, to be sure.

I certainly hope that it won't occur to him that the play, one of the merriest that could be staged, is written without the slightest ambiguity, without a thought or a single word which might offend the modesty of young girls in the boxes, an accomplishment that is certainly something, sir, in a century when hypocrisy about decency is pushed almost to the point of abandoning moral standards. With the greatest pleasure. No doubt, all this is something to which the attention of such a major critic could not stoop.

But how could he not admire what no good people can see without shedding tender tears of pleasure? I mean the filial piety of that good Figaro, who never can forget his mother.

"Do you know her guardian?" the Count asked him in the first act. "Like my own mother," Figaro replies. A miser would have said, "Like my purse"; a fop would have replied, "Like myself"; an opportunist, "Like the way to Versailles"; and the journalist of Bouillon, "Like my library." Each one draws his comparison invariably from the object that interests him. "Like my own mother," said the tender and respectful son.

In yet another passage, "How nice you look," the guardian says to him. And this good honest fellow, who can blithely take this compliment along with all those he has received from his mistresses, always comes back to his good mother. He replies to the remark, how nice, "Sir, it's true that my mother used to tell me that." And the newspaper in Bouillon doesn't notice traits like that! One's brain must be altogether dried up not to see them, or the heart quite hard not to feel them.

Not to mention a thousand other fine artistic points spread openhandedly over the whole work. For example, it's well known that the acting profession has developed an infinity of special types: the great, the medium, and the small lover; the great, the medium and the small valet; the simpleton, the man of affairs, the countryman, the peasant, the notary, the bailiff. But it's also well known that they have never specialized in a man who yawns. What came over the author to train an actor with little practice in the art to open his mouth wide on the stage? He took the trouble to put together for him in a single phrase all the yawning syllables in French: *rien, qu'en, l'en, t'en, dant, parler*—syllables which would certainly make a dead man yawn, and would even succeed in relaxing the jaws of envy!

In this admirable passage, the barber is reproached by the guardian, who shouts at him, "What have you to say to that poor wretch who yawns and sleeps when he's wide awake? And to that other one who has sneezed enough in the past three hours to crack his skull and blow his brains out? What have you to say to them?" And the naive barber replies, "Oh, well, to the one who sneezes I'll say, 'God bless you,' and 'Go to bed' to the one who yawns." A reply, to be sure, that is so right, so Christian, and so admirable that one of these proud critics whose entry into Paradise is already assured cannot forbear exclaiming, "Gad! the author must have taken at least eight days to find that reply!"

And the newspaper of Bouillon, instead of praising these countless beauties, uses ink and paper, consent and privilege, to put such a work beneath criticism! My throat would have to be cut, sir, before I could keep silent about it!

Hasn't that cruel fellow gone so far as to say "that in order to keep this barber from dying on the stage it had to be mutilated, altered, recast, cut, reduced to four acts, and purged of a great many lampoons, puns, and plays on words, in short, of low comedy?

By the way he beats it so unmercifully, one is led to suspect that he hasn't understood the first word of the play that he is tearing apart. But I have the honor to inform this journalist, as well as the young man who mends his pens and his writing, that, far from purging the play of any puns, plays on words, etc., that might have marred its first performance, the author had to restore to the script used for the stage all that he had saved up in his portfolio, just the way an economical carpenter searches out among the scattered chips in his lumberyard anything that might plug and stop the smallest holes in his work.

Shall we pass over in silence the shrill reproach that he gave his leading lady *all the faults of a badly brought-up girl?* It's true that, to escape the consequences of such an imputation, he attempts to attribute this opinion to others, as if it weren't his own, by using that banal expression *it is felt that the young lady,* etc. It is felt!

What do you want her to do then? What? Instead of accommodating herself to the desires of a very amiable young lover who also proves to be a man of quality, our charming child should marry the old gouty doctor? A fine arrangement that would be for her! And because she does not share that gentleman's opinion, *she has all the faults of a badly brought-up girl!*

I'm sure that if the paper of Bouillon makes friends in France by the justice and candor of its criticisms, we must allow that it will make far fewer of them on the other side of the Pyrenees, and that above all it's pretty hard on the Spanish ladies.

Ah, who knows if Her Excellency the Countess Almaviva, the paragon of women in her circle, who lives like an angel with her husband even though she no longer loves him, will not one day resent the liberties that are taken with her at Bouillon, with consent and privilege?

Has the imprudent journalist ever reflected that Her Excellency has, because of her husband's rank, great credit at court; she could obtain a place for him on the Spanish Gazette, or even on her own Gazette. When he takes up that career, he will have to use more discretion in speaking of ladies of quality. What's all this to me? It's obvious that I speak only for his own good.

It's time to forget this adversary, even if he is at the head of the party that maintains that, *not being able to sustain five acts, I restricted myself to four in order to keep my public.* And what if I did? In a moment of crisis isn't it better to sacrifice a fifth of your goods than to see all of them destroyed?

But don't fall, dear reader—sir, I mean to say—don't

fall, I beg you, into a vulgar error which would greatly damage your reputation for good judgment.

Although my play appears today to be in only four acts, it is actually and in truth in five, which are the first, the second, the third, the fourth, and the fifth, as usual.

It is true that, on the day of battle, seeing the enemy aroused, the audience undulating, heaving, growling in the distance like the waves of the sea, and quite convinced that these dull roarings, the harbingers of tempests, had preceded more than one shipwreck, it occurred to me that a great many plays in five acts (like mine), all very well written besides (like mine), would not have gone altogether to pieces (like mine), if the author had taken a drastic step (like mine).

The gods of the opposition being irritated, I cried valiantly to the actors, "Boys! A sacrifice is needed here." Then, giving up a part to save the rest and tearing my manuscript: "God of hissers, nose-blowers, spitters, coughers, and disturbers," I exclaimed, "you need blood; drink my fourth act, and may it appease your fury!"

At that instant you might have seen the infernal noise which made the actors stumble and grow pale, abate, move off, fade away. It was succeeded by a cheer, and from the depths of the auditorium a general *bravo* arose and circled the topmost galleries.

From this explanation, sir, it follows that my play remains in five acts, which are the first, the second, the third on the stage, the fourth to the devil, and the fifth with three in front of it. Even the author himself maintains that this unseen fourth act is not the least contribution to the greatness of the play, just because it is unseen.

Let people prate; it's enough for me that I've proved my statement. It's enough for me that, by writing my five acts, I have paid my respects to Aristotle, Horace, Aubignac, and the moderns, and have concealed the honor I paid to the rule.

By the second arrangement, the devil has his due; my cart rolls no worse without the fifth wheel; the public is happy, and I am too. Why isn't the newspaper in Bouillon? Ah, why? Because it's very difficult to please people who, by profession, are bound never to find merry things serious enough, nor serious things merry enough.

I flatter myself, sir, that this is called arguing principles, and that you will not mind my little syllogism.

It remains to reply to certain observations with which certain persons have honored the least important play that has appeared in our theater in a century.

I set apart the letters written to the actors and even to me without a signature and vulgarly called *anonymous*. One judges from the asperity of the style that their authors, little versed in criticism, have too little sense of the fact that a bad play is not a bad deed, and that the abuse suitable for a bad man is out of place to a bad author. Let us pass on to others.

Some experts have remarked that I committed the fault of allowing French customs to be criticized by a jester of Seville, in Seville, whereas verisimilitude requires that he hold forth on Spanish customs. They are right; I even planned at first, in order to render the verisimilitude still more perfect, to write and have the play performed in Spanish. But a man of taste observed to me that it might perhaps lose a little of its sparkle for the public in Paris, a reason that decided me to write in French, with the result that I made, as you can see, a multitude of sacrifices for the sake of merriment, without succeeding in cheering up the newspaper in Bouillon.

Another amateur, seizing a moment when the lobby was crowded, reproached me in the most serious tone with the fact that my play resembled *You Can't Think of Everything*. "Resembles, sir? I maintain that my play is *You Can't Think of Everything*." "And how is that?" "Because they have not yet thought about my play." The amateur stopped short, and there was all the more laughter because the man who reproached me with *You Can't Think of Everything* is a man who has never thought of anything.

Some days later (this is more serious) at the home of an invalid lady, a sober gentleman dressed in black, with a puffed headdress and an ebony cane with which he lightly touched the lady's wrist, politely offers many doubts of the truth of the charges I have thrown against doctors. "Sir," I say to him, "are you a friend of one of them? I would hate to think that a joke—" "No one could be less so. I see that you don't know me; I never take anyone's part. I speak only of the profession in general." That sets me to wondering what man this could be. "When it comes to humor," I replied, "you know, sir, that no one ever asks if the story is true, but only if it is good." "Oh, do you think you can pass that test any better than the first?" "Well done, doctor," said the lady. "Monster that he is, he has dared to speak ill of us women too. Let's make common cause against him."

At this word *doctor*, I began to suspect that it was her physician she spoke to. "It's true, sir and madam," I replied modestly, "that I permit myself these little liberties the more easily, the less serious their consequences appear. Well! Who could harm two powerful bodies whose empire embraces the universe and who share the world between them? In spite of their detractors, the girls rule by pleasure and the doctors by pain; glowing health leads us back to love as sickness leads us back to the doctor. Nevertheless, I am not certain whether, in the balance of power, the doctors don't outweigh the girls a little. The girls often send us to the doctors, but more often still the doctors keep us and don't send us back to the girls.

"While joking then, it would be well to keep an eye on the difference between their two methods of attack: to recall that if the girls seek revenge by abandoning us, it's only a negative evil; whereas the doctors seek revenge by taking possession of us, an evil that is quite positive.

"That when the latter take us, they make out of us whatever they choose; whereas the girls, beautiful as they are, make of us only what they can.

"That intercourse with the girls soon renders them less necessary to us; whereas the employment of a doctor ends by his becoming indispensable to us.

"Finally, that one of these empires appears to be established only to support the other, seeing that the more the green youth is given over to love, the more surely the pale old man belongs to the doctor.

"Moreover, having made common cause against me, it was fair, madam and sir, that I offer you my justification in common. Be assured that when I use my adoration of the girls and my fear of the doctors in my writing, it's always in jest that I speak badly of the girls, and it's never without trembling that I make a little fun of medicine.

"With respect to you, ladies, my declaration is not suspect. My bitterest enemies are forced to admit that when I, in a temperamental mood, am sufficiently piqued at some girl to unbosom myself too freely about all the others, I am known to stop short at the twenty-fifth verse and, with the promptest repentance in the twenty-sixth, to make honorable amends this way to the ruffled ladies:

> Lovely girls, if I reveal
> That joy is all you ever treasure,
> Though love you very seldom feel,
> You are faithful to your pleasure;
> Don't seek to hit me in your turn
> For the mischief that I do.
> The man who jokes can also burn
> From weaknesses he shares with you.

"As for you, doctor, everyone knows that Molière—"

"I regret," he says as he rises, "that I am unable to profit further from your insights, but groaning humanity must not be left to suffer for my pleasures." He leaves me, on my word, with my mouth open and my words in the air. "I don't know," says the beautiful invalid, laughing, "whether I pardon you, but it's clear that our doctor doesn't." "Ours, madam? He will never be mine." "Why not?" "I don't know; I would be afraid that he was not quite up to his position, since he is not above the pleasantries that are made about it.

"This doctor does not attend me. The man sufficiently perfect in his art to admit its uncertitude in good faith, witty enough to laugh with me at those who believe themselves infallible, he is my doctor. By rendering me the attentions that he calls visits, by giving me the advice that he calls prescriptions, he fulfills with dignity and without ostentation the noblest function of a sensible and enlightened being. The more intelligent he is, the more money he makes, and that's all one can do in an art that is as useful as it is uncertain. He examines me, he consoles me, he directs me, and nature does the rest. Besides, far from being offended by humor, he's the first to use it against pedantry. A fatuous person says to him, 'I treated eighty inflamed lungs this autumn, and only one patient died in my hands.' My doctor replies with a smile, 'As for me, I've lent my aid to more than a hundred this winter; alas, I've been able to cover up only one.' Such is my friendly doctor."

"I know him." "Forgive me if I don't exchange him for yours. A pedant has no more of my confidence in sickness than a prude receives of my homage in health. But what a fool I am! Instead of running through the verse that makes amends to the fair sex, I should have sung him the verse about the prude; it suits him perfectly:

> I gather sketches here and there
> To use to make a witty scene;
> No more than fancy, to be fair,
> A portrait isn't what I mean.
> The wise man wears a little smile;
> "How true that is," he will say.
> The man who thinks that I revile,
> By anger gives himself away."

"Speaking of songs," said the lady, "it was good of you to give your play to the French actors. I take a *petite loge* only to see the Italians. Why didn't you make it a comic opera? They say you intended to at first. It's the kind of play that's suited to music."

"I don't know if it's suited, or whether I was mistaken to think so at first. Without going into the reasons that made me change my mind, these, madam, may serve.

"Our dramatic music is still too much like our songs to provide any true interest or fresh merriment. We should begin to use music seriously in the theater, to use it only when we feel strongly that it is better to sing than to speak. And our musicians must get closer to nature; above all, they must stop insisting on their absurd law of always repeating the first part of an air after completing the second. Are there reprises and rondos in drama? This cruel nonsense kills every bit of interest, and it indicates an insupportable dearth of ideas.

"I have always adored music, faithfully, and even without infidelity. But often, even with the pieces that I enjoy most, I catch myself shrugging a shoulder and saying quietly and with good humor, 'Oh, go on, music! Why repeat all the time? Aren't you slow enough? Instead of telling your story quickly, you maunder on and on! Instead of portraying passion, you linger over the words! The poet kills himself to hasten the issue, and you dawdle! What use is it for him to cultivate an energetic, swift style if you bury it under useless trills? While you display such a sterile abundance, take all your nourishment from our songs, until you learn the sublime and tumultuous language of the passions.'

"For that matter, if declamation is itself an abuse of narration on the stage, singing, which is an abuse of declamation, becomes an abuse of an abuse. Add to that the repetition of phrases and see what happens to your interest. While the fault is ever increasing, the interest moves in the opposite direction; the action flags; something fails me; I become distracted; boredom overcomes me; and if I try to find out what I want, I often find that I want the end of the show.

"Another imitative art, in general much less advanced than music, is able to give a lesson in this respect. Taken only in regard to variety, classical dancing is an excellent model for singing.

"Watch the superb Vestris or the magnificent d'Auberval begin a character dance. Even before he's dancing, from the first moment you see him, his free and easy bearing causes the spectators to lift their heads. He breathes as much pride as he promises of pleasure. He is gone . . . While the musician repeats his phrases twenty times and the monotony of his movements, the dancer varies his infinitely.

"Watch him as he advances lightly with little leaps, draws back in long steps, and conceals the utmost in artistry by the appearance of ease. Sometimes on one foot, maintaining the most intricate balance, suspended motionless through several measures, he astonishes and surprises us by the immobility of his equilibrium . . . And suddenly, as if he regretted the time of repose, he goes like a swallow, flies to the back of the stage, and returns in pirouettes with a rapidity that the eye can scarcely follow.

"In vain the music goes back to the beginning, does a rigadoon, repeats itself, chatters idly to itself—he doesn't repeat, not he! At the same time he is displaying the virile beauty of his supple and powerful body, he portrays the violent movements which stir the soul; he shoots a passionate glance at you that is rendered more expressive by his open, indolent arms; and, as if he soon tired of pleasing you, he draws back with disdain, hiding from the eye that follows him, and the most fiery passion seems to arise from, to emerge from the sweetest rapture. Impetuous, turbulent, he expresses an anger so boiling and so true that he draws me out of my seat and makes me knit my brows. Then, suddenly resuming the accent and the gesture of peaceful delight, he roves about nonchalantly with a grace, an indolence, and with movements so delicate that he carries away as many votes as there are people watching his enchanting dance."

Composers, sing as he dances, and we will have, instead of operas, melodramas! But I hear my eternal censor (I don't know any longer whether he's from somewhere else or from Bouillon) who says to me: "What do you mean by this description? I see here a superior talent, not the dance in general. You must take an art in its ordinary manifestations if you want to compare it, and not in its most sublime aspects. Have we not—"

It's my turn to interrupt. What do you mean? If I want to portray a charger and form for myself a true idea of this noble animal, will I go to one that is gelded and old, groaning alongside the pole of a coach, or ambling along under the whistling lime seller? I'll rather go to the stud farm, to find a fierce stallion, vigorous, untrammeled, with an ardent eye, pounding the earth and breathing fire from his nostrils, bounding with eagerness and impatience, splitting the air while he electrifies it, and whose brusque neighing is the delight of man and makes all the mares in the county tremble with pleasure. Such is my dancer.

"And when I describe an art, I intend to select my models from among its great practitioners. All the efforts of a genius . . . But I'm going too far with this subject; let's return to *The Barber of Seville* . . . or rather, sir, let's not return to it. This is enough for such a trifle. Unwittingly I will succumb to the fault so justly charged against us French, of always making little ditties about great matters and long dissertations about small ones."

I am, with the most profound respect,

Sir,

Your very humble
and most obedient servant,

The Author

THE BARBER OF SEVILLE

THE CHARACTERS

(All the actors are costumed in the old Spanish style.)

Count Almaviva, *a Spanish nobleman,* rosine's *secret lover.*

In the first act, he wears a satin jacket and breeches; he is wrapped in a large brown mantle, or Spanish cape, wears a black hat turned down, with a colored ribbon around the crown. In the second act, a cavalier's uniform, with moustaches and half-boots. In the third act, a scholar's costume, with round hair and a large ruff on his neck; the jacket, breeches, stockings, and mantle of a priest. In the fourth act, he wears a superb suit in the Spanish style, with a rich mantle; over it he wears a large brown mantle to keep it hidden.

Bartholo, *a doctor,* rosine's *guardian.*

He wears a black costume, short and buttoned, a large wig, standing ruff and cuffs, a black sash, and, when he leaves the house, a long scarlet mantle.

Rosine, *a young lady of noble birth,* bartholo's *ward.*

Her dress is in the Spanish style.

Figaro, *a barber of Seville.*

He dresses as a Spanish majo. *His head is covered*

1

with a net; he has a white hat with a colored ribbon around the crown, a silk neckerchief worn loosely around his neck, satin waistcoat and breeches with buttons and buttonholes edged in silver, a wide silk sash, knotted garters with tassels that hang down his legs, a bright-colored jacket with a broad facing matching the waistcoat, white stockings and gray shoes.

DON BAZILE, *an organist,* ROSINE'S *singing teacher.*
He wears a black hat turned down, a short cassock and long mantle, without ruff or cuffs.

THE BOY, *an old servant of* BARTHOLO.

BRIGHT-EYES, *another servant of* BARTHOLO, *a silly sleepy boy.*
Both servants are dressed as Galicians. All the hair is in a queue, a chamois-colored waistcoat, a large leather belt with a buckle, blue breeches and jacket, with the sleeves hanging down the back and the arms appearing through a slit at the shoulder.

A NOTARY.

THE ALCALDE, *a justice of the peace, with a long white stick in his hand.*

SEVERAL POLICEMEN AND SERVANTS WITH TORCHES.

The scene of the play is Seville: in the first act, in the street under ROSINE'S *window, the rest of the play in* DOCTOR BARTHOLO'S *house.*

THE BARBER OF SEVILLE

Act I

(The stage represents a street in Seville; all the windows of the houses are barred. The Count *is discovered alone, wearing a large brown mantle and a hat with the brim turned down. He paces back and forth and looks at his watch.)*

Count. It's earlier than I thought. It's nowhere near the time when she usually appears behind the blinds. Never mind; I'd rather be here too soon than risk missing my one chance to see her. If any of my court friends could see me here, a hundred leagues from Madrid, waiting every morning under the window of a girl I've never spoken to, he would take me for a romantic old Spaniard of Isabella's time. Why not? Everybody wants happiness; mine is in Rosine's heart. But after all, to follow a woman to Seville, when in Madrid and at the court easy pleasures are always at hand—? And that's exactly what I've run away from. I'm tired of conquests prompted by intrigue, greed, and vanity. It's so sweet to be loved for yourself! If I can only be sure that this disguise— The devil take this intruder!

3

(The Count *hides as* Figaro *enters, a guitar fastened on his back by a broad ribbon. He hums merrily, a pencil and paper in his hand.)*

Figaro.

> Now banish all care
> That eats at the heart;
> Good wine, I declare,
> 20   Will make it depart.
> The man without joy
> Himself will destroy;
> Like a beast he will try
> To live till he die.

There! That's not so bad! What do you think?

> To live till he die.
> Idleness and wine
> Fight for my heart—

Oh, no, they're not fighting. They get along there very
30 well together.

> Share in my heart—

Share in? What kind of talk is that? Oh, well, people
who write comic operas aren't fussy about these
things. Nowadays, if it's hardly worth speaking, you
sing it.

> Idleness and wine
> Share in my heart.

Now I ought to finish with a great burst, something
sparkling, brilliant, something like an epigram. *(He
kneels on one knee and writes while he sings.)*
40   Share in my heart;
> One makes me feel fine,

The other helps my art.

No, that's flat! That won't do. I need a contrast, an antithesis.

One's—a mistress fine,

The other—

Ah! That'll do it!

The other's a sweetheart.

Very good, Figaro. (*He writes while he sings.*)

Idleness and wine   50

Share in my heart.

One's a mistress fine,

The other's a sweetheart,

The other's a sweetheart,

The other's a sweetheart.

There, you see? Wait till I put an accompaniment to this; then those scheming intriguers will see whether or not I know what I'm talking about. (*He sees the* COUNT.) I've seen that abbot somewhere before.

COUNT. That man looks familiar.   60

FIGARO. He's no abbot. That proud and noble bearing—

COUNT. That grotesque figure—

FIGARO. I can't be mistaken. That's Count Almaviva.

COUNT. It must be that rascal Figaro.

FIGARO. That's who I am, milord.

COUNT. Idiot! If you speak a single word—

FIGARO. Yes, I recognize you all right. You're treating me with your usual courtesy.

COUNT. Well, I'd hardly know you. You're so slick 70 and so thick—

FIGARO. Can't be helped, sir. Times are bad.

COUNT. Poor fellow! But what are you doing in Seville? Not long ago I recommended you for a government job.

FIGARO. I got it, milord, and my gratitude—

COUNT. Call me Lindor. Can't you tell from my disguise that I don't want to be recognized?

FIGARO. I'd better leave you.

80   COUNT. By no means. I have to wait here, and two men chatting are less suspicious than one man walking up and down alone. Just look as if we're chatting. Well, how about this job?

FIGARO. Thanks to Your Excellency's recommendation, the minister immediately appointed me an assistant apothecary.

COUNT. In the army hospital?

FIGARO. No, at the stud farm in Andalusia.

COUNT. (*Laughing*) That's a good start!

90   FIGARO. It wasn't a bad job. Since I was in charge of the cures and drugs, sometimes I could sell good horse medicine to men.

COUNT. Thereby killing off the King's subjects.

FIGARO. Oh, well, there's no universal remedy. Sometimes even the best medicine won't cure a stevedore.

COUNT. Then why did you give it up?

FIGARO. Give it up? It gave me up. Somebody denounced me to the authorities. "Envy, with crooked

100 fingers, a pale and livid face—"

COUNT. Oh, come now, my friend. Do you write verses too? I've been watching you scribbling there on your knee and singing all morning.

Figaro. That's precisely the cause of my troubles, sir. When the minister heard that I was offering, I think I can say pretty good poetical bouquets to Cloris, that I sent riddles to the papers, that my style of madrigal was all the rage—in a word, when he learned that I was breaking out in print all over the place, he took a tragic view of the situation and threw me out of my job, on the ground that a love of letters is incompatible with a businesslike attitude.

Count. That's powerful thinking! And didn't you point out to him—?

Figaro. I considered myself lucky to be forgotten. I figure that a great man does us enough good when he does us no harm.

Count. That's not the whole story. I remember when you were in my service you were none too good.

Figaro. Oh, good heavens, sir, you want a poor man to be perfect.

Count. Lazy, troublesome—

Figaro. If you judge masters by the virtues you expect in their servants, does Your Excellency know many who are worthy of being valets?

Count. (*Laughing*) Not bad! So you came to this city?

Figaro. Not right away.

Count. (*Interrupting*) One moment. I thought I heard her. (*The* Count *watches the window closely.*) Go on talking. I can hear you well enough.

Figaro. On my return to Madrid, I thought I'd try my literary talents again. The theater looked like a worthy field of honor—

COUNT. Oh, what a pity! (*He continues to watch the window closely.*)

FIGARO. To tell the truth, I don't know why I wasn't a tremendous success. I filled the pit with a fine lot of workmen with hands like paddles; I forbade all gloves, canes, and anything else that might interfere with
140 loud applause; and I must say that before the performance the crowd in the cafe seemed well disposed toward me. But then somebody organized the opposition—

COUNT. Organized opposition! The author must have failed.

FIGARO. Why can't I use that excuse? Everybody else does. They hissed me. But if ever I get them together again—

COUNT. You'll revenge yourself by boring them?

150 FIGARO. I have terrible plans for them, by God!

COUNT. You're swearing! Don't you know that the courts allow only twenty-four hours to swear at the judge?

FIGARO. In the theater you have twenty-four years. Life is too short to use up all that resentment.

COUNT. You have a witty anger, anyway. But you haven't told me why you left Madrid.

FIGARO. My good angel must have led me here, Your Excellency, since I'm lucky enough to come across my
160 old master. I found out that the literary circles in Madrid are like packs of wolves, constantly on guard against each other, and when they fall into the contempt that their silly obstinacy brings them to, then

all the insects—gnats, mosquitoes, critics, jealous people, hack writers, booksellers, censors, and all the others that latch onto the skins of poor writers—they manage to tear and bleed what little substance is left for them. Tired of writing, bored with myself, disgusted with others, sunk in debt and unburdened with money, finally convinced that the real revenue from my razor is preferable to the empty honor of my pen, I left Madrid. With my baggage on my back, I wandered philosophically through the two Castiles, La Mancha, Estremadura, Sierra Morena, and Andalusia—hailed in one town and jailed in the next, and rising above both, wherever I was; praised by some, blamed by others, enjoying the good weather and enduring the bad; mocking the fools and defying the wicked, laughing off misery and bearding everybody, now you find me settled in Seville and ready once more to serve Your Excellency in anything you care to undertake.

COUNT. What gave you such a happy outlook?

FIGARO. Growing accustomed to misfortune. I'm quick to laugh at everything for fear that I might weep. What are you staring at over there?

COUNT. Let's get out of here.

FIGARO. Why?

COUNT. Come on, you wretch! You'll ruin me!

(*They hide. The shutter on the second floor opens and* BARTHOLO *and* ROSINE *appear at the window.*)

ROSINE. What a pleasure it is to breathe fresh air! This shutter is hardly ever open.

BARTHOLO. What's that paper you have there?

ROSINE. A few verses from *The Useless Precaution* that my singing teacher gave me yesterday.

BARTHOLO. What's *The Useless Precaution*?

ROSINE. It's a new comedy.

BARTHOLO. One of those new-fangled plays! Some new kind of foolishness.

ROSINE. I don't know anything about it.

200 BARTHOLO. Well, anyhow, the critics and the authorities will see that justice is done. What a barbarous age!

ROSINE. You're always complaining about our poor age.

BARTHOLO. Pardon me for taking such a liberty. What has it produced that's worth praising? Every kind of nonsense: free thought, the law of gravity, magnetism, religious tolerance, inoculation, quinine, the Encyclopedia, and new plays—

(ROSINE *drops the paper; it falls into the street.*)

ROSINE. Oh, my song! I dropped my song while I was listening to you! Run, run down quickly, sir! My song
210 —it will be lost!

BARTHOLO. What a nuisance! Why don't you hold onto things?

(*He leaves the balcony.* ROSINE, *looking back into the room, signals to the street.*)

ROSINE. Pst, pst!

(*The* COUNT *comes out of hiding.*)

Pick it up quickly and get away!

(*The* COUNT *picks up the paper in one jump and hides*

again. BARTHOLO *comes out of the house and looks about.*)

BARTHOLO. Where is it? I don't see anything.

ROSINE. Under the balcony, close to the wall.

BARTHOLO. This is a nice job you've given me. Has anyone passed by?

ROSINE. I haven't seen anyone.

BARTHOLO. (*To himself*) Why am I so foolish as to   220
look for it? Bartholo, my friend, you're nothing but a dolt. This ought to teach you never to open the window on the street. (*He goes back into the house.*)

ROSINE. (*On the balcony*) My excuse is that I'm so unhappy. I'm a lonely prisoner, the victim of that odious man's persecution. Is it a crime to try to escape from slavery?

BARTHOLO. (*Appearing on the balcony*) Come in, señora. It's my fault that you lost your song, but I assure you that such a misfortune will not happen again.   230

(*He closes and locks the shutter.* FIGARO *and the* COUNT *come stealthily out of hiding.*)

COUNT. Now that they've gone, let's take a look at this song. There must be some secret in it. It's a note!

FIGARO. He wanted to know what *The Useless Precaution* is!

COUNT (*Reading excitedly*) "Your devotion excites my curiosity. As soon as my guardian goes out, sing in an offhand way to the tune of these verses and let me learn at last the name, the rank and the intentions of the man who appears to be so desperately attached to the unfortunate Rosine."   240

FIGARO. (*Imitating* ROSINE's *voice*) Oh, my song! I dropped my song! Run, run down quickly! (*He laughs.*) Oh, these women! Do you know how to turn the most innocent girl into a sly minx? Lock her up.

COUNT. My sweet Rosine!

FIGARO. Now I see the reason for your masquerade, sir. You have love on your mind.

COUNT. That's it. But if you chatter—

FIGARO. Me, chatter? I won't try to convince you of
250 my discretion in those high-flown terms that everybody takes in vain every day. I'll just say this: my own interests will make me a reliable man for you. Weigh everything in that scale and—

COUNT. Good enough. Then let me explain that I happened to meet in the Prado, about six months ago, such a beautiful young lady—Well, you've just seen her. I searched for her all over Madrid in vain. Only a few days ago I discovered that her name is Rosine, she's of noble blood, an orphan, and married to an old
260 doctor here named Bartholo.

FIGARO. A pretty bird, I must say, and hard to pull out of the nest. But who told you she's the doctor's wife?

COUNT. Everybody.

FIGARO. That's only the story he spread around when he came here from Madrid, to mislead the young men and keep them away. She's still only his ward, but soon—

COUNT. (*Excitedly*) Never! Oh, what news! I was
270 ready to run any risk just to let her know of my disappointment, and now I find she's free! There's not a

moment to lose! I must win her love and rescue her from that disgusting alliance he plans for her. Do you know her guardian?

FIGARO. Like my own mother.

COUNT. What sort of man is he?

FIGARO. (*Merrily*) He's a fine great, short, young old man, dapple gray, torn, shorn, worn, who peeps and pries, grumbles and mumbles all at the same time.

COUNT. (*Impatiently*) Oh, I know what he looks 280 like. What's his disposition?

FIGARO. Brutal, grasping, enamored, and jealous beyond all measure of his ward, who hates him like poison.

COUNT. Then his chances of pleasing her are—?

FIGARO. Invisible.

COUNT. So much the better. Is he honest?

FIGARO. Only just enough to escape hanging.

COUNT. So much the better. To punish a rogue while gaining my own happiness—   290

FIGARO. That's creating public and personal good at the same time. A masterpiece of morality, I must say, sir.

COUNT. You said that his fear of young men makes him keep his doors locked?

FIGARO. Yes, against everybody. And if he knew how to stop up the cracks—

COUNT. So much the worse. There isn't any chance of your getting into the house?

FIGARO. Any chance! *Primo,* the house where I live 300 belongs to the doctor. He lets me have it *gratis.*

COUNT. Ah, ha!

FIGARO. Yes. And in gratitude I promise him ten gold pistoles a year, also *gratis*.

COUNT. (*Impatiently*) So you're his tenant?

FIGARO. More. I'm his barber, his surgeon, his apothecary. In his house there's never a stroke of the razor, the lancet, or the syringe from any hand but this of your servant.

310 COUNT. (*Embracing him*) Figaro, my friend! You'll be my angel, my liberator, my guiding spirit!

FIGARO. Bah! How quickly my usefulness endears me to you! Don't tell me about men in love!

COUNT. You lucky Figaro! You're going to see my Rosine! You're going to see her! Do you realize how lucky you are?

FIGARO. There's love talking! Am I in love with her? I wish you could take my place.

COUNT. Oh, if we could only get the guards out of
320 the house.

FIGARO. That's what I was thinking.

COUNT. Just for twelve hours.

FIGARO. If we keep the servants busy with their own affairs, they can't interfere in other people's affairs.

COUNT. No doubt. So?

FIGARO. (*Pondering*) I'm trying to think of some harmless medical device to—

COUNT. You villain!

FIGARO. You don't think I'd hurt them? They all need
330 my attentions. The only problem is how to treat them all at the same time.

COUNT. But the doctor might be suspicious.

FIGARO. We must work quickly, before there's time

for suspicion to arise. I have an idea: the Prince's regiment is coming to the city.

COUNT. The colonel is a friend of mine.

FIGARO. Good. Present yourself at the doctor's house
in a soldier's uniform, with a billet for lodging. He'll
have to take you in. Then leave the rest to me.

COUNT. Wonderful!   340

FIGARO. It would be even better if you were a little
drunk—

COUNT. What for?

FIGARO. And put on rough manners under that pretense.

COUNT. What for?

FIGARO. To prevent his suspicions, to make him believe you're more anxious to sleep than to carry on in-
trigues in his house.

COUNT. Well taken! But won't you be there?   350

FIGARO. Oh, yes, me! We'll be pretty lucky if he
doesn't recognize you, whom he has never seen. And
how could I introduce you later?

COUNT. You're right.

FIGARO. I wonder if you can keep up this difficult
part—a cavalier, a bit unsteady—

COUNT. You're joking. (*Putting on a drunken voice*)
Isn't this here Doctor Bartholo's house, my friend?

FIGARO. Not bad, I must say. A little more wine in
the legs. (*In a more drunken voice*) Isn't this here   360
house—

COUNT. Oh, no, that's a vulgar drunk.

FIGARO. It's a good one, and very pleasant.

COUNT. The door's opening!

FIGARO. There's our man. Let's hide again until he's gone.

(*They hide as* BARTHOLO *comes out, speaking to someone inside.*)

BARTHOLO. I'll be back soon. Don't let anyone in. What a fool I was to come down! I should have known better as soon as she asked me to. Why hasn't Bazile come? He should have everything arranged for my secret marriage tomorrow, and I hear no news! I'm going to find out what's keeping him.

(*He goes off. The* COUNT *and* FIGARO *come out of hiding.*)

COUNT. What's that he said? Tomorrow he's going to marry Rosine secretly!

FIGARO. Well, sir, the difficulty of succeeding merely increases the necessity to try.

COUNT. Who is this Bazile that's meddling with his marriage?

FIGARO. A poor creature who teaches music to his ward. He's infatuated with his art, a sly rascal, a beggar who falls on his knees before a piece of gold. He'll be easy to manage, sir. (*Looking at the window*) There she is! There she is!

COUNT. Who is it?

FIGARO. Behind the shutter—there she is! There she is! Don't look! Don't look now!

COUNT. Why not?

FIGARO. Don't you remember? She wrote, "Sing in

an offhand way." She means to sing—to nobody, just
for the fun of it. Oh, there she is, there she is!   390

COUNT. Since she's already interested without knowing who I am, I'll keep the disguise of Lindor. My triumph will be all the sweeter. (*He opens the paper
that* ROSINE *threw from the window.*) But how can I
sing to this music? I'm no good at making verses.

FIGARO. Anything that comes to you, sir, will be just
right. A lover's heart isn't critical. And take my guitar.

COUNT. What can I do with it? I play so badly.

FIGARO. Is there anything a man like you can't do?
With the back of your hand, tum, tum, tum. To sing   400
without a guitar in Seville! You'd be noticed right away
and unmasked. (FIGARO *glues himself to the wall under the balcony.*)

COUNT. (*Singing as he walks back and forth, accom-
panying himself on the guitar*)

> I have received an order from your hand;
> To adore you from afar was all too bold.
> What may I hope when all the truth is told?
> But I must speak it out when you command.

FIGARO. (*Quietly*) Very good indeed! Keep it up, sir!

COUNT.

> I am Lindor, of lowly rank and birth,
> A student quite unknown to worldly fame.
> Ah! would I had a noble knight's great name   410
> To offer you the glory you are worth.

FIGARO. Oh, what the devil! I pride myself on this,
and I couldn't do any better!

COUNT.

> Each morning here I'll sing you of my love

In tender phrases, all forlorn of hope,
Asking no more than here below to grope,
While you all glorious listen from above.

FIGARO. Oh, my word! That last verse—! (*He comes forward and kisses the hem of the* COUNT'S *cloak.*)

COUNT. Figaro!

420   FIGARO. Your Excellency?

COUNT. Do you think she might have heard me?

ROSINE. (*Singing, inside*)

Everything speaks to me of Lindor's charm
And tells me I should love him faithfully—

(*A window is heard to close sharply.*)

FIGARO. Now do you think she might have heard you?

COUNT. She closed her window. Someone must have come into the room.

FIGARO. Oh, the poor little thing. She was trembling when she sang! She's yours, sir.

430   COUNT. She replied to me the same way!

Everything speaks to me of Lindor's charm.
What grace! What cleverness!

FIGARO. What tricks! What love!

COUNT. Do you think she'll come with me, Figaro?

FIGARO. She'd rather pass through that window than not.

COUNT. It's all over! I belong to Rosine—for life!

FIGARO. Sir, you're forgetting that she's not listening now.

440   COUNT. Figaro, I have only one thing to say to you: she is to be my wife. And if you serve me well in this

matter by keeping my name a secret—you understand me, you know me.

FIGARO. I'm with you. There you are, Figaro; your fortune's made, my lad.

COUNT. Let's go before someone suspects us.

FIGARO. As for me, I'll go in here and use all the tricks of my trade in one master stroke, to disarm vigilance, awaken love, mislead jealousy, baffle schemes, and overcome all obstacles. You, sir, at my house, in a 450 soldier's uniform, with an order for lodging, and money in your pockets.

COUNT. What's the money for?

FIGARO. Money, good lord, money! That's what makes schemes work.

COUNT. Don't get upset, Figaro. I'll have plenty.

FIGARO. (*Starting off*) I'll be with you right away.

COUNT. Figaro!

FIGARO. What is it?

COUNT. What about your guitar?   460

FIGARO. I forgot my guitar! How could I? I'm losing my wits. (*He starts to go again.*)

COUNT. Where is your house, you idiot?

FIGARO. (*Coming back*) Oh, I'm really out of my mind! My shop four steps from here, painted blue, leaded windows, three pans hanging up, an eye in a hand—*Consilio manuque*, FIGARO! (*He runs off.*)

Act II

❧

(*The stage represents* ROSINE's *room. The window at the back is closed with a grilled shutter.* ROSINE *is alone, with a candlestick in her hand. She sits at a table, takes paper, and starts to write.*)

ROSINE. Marceline is ill, and all the servants are busy; no one sees me writing. I don't know whether these walls have eyes and ears, or whether my Argus has some evil spirit that warns him just at the wrong time, but I can't take a step or speak a word without his knowing what I'm up to on the spot. Ah, Lindor! (*She seals the letter.*) My letter is sealed anyhow, even though I have no idea when or how I can get it to him. When I watched him through the shutter, I saw him talking for a long time to the barber Figaro. That good man is sometimes sympathetic with me; if I could manage to speak to him for a moment—

(FIGARO *enters, to* ROSINE's *surprise.*)

Oh, Master Figaro! How glad I am to see you!

FIGARO. How are you, my lady?

ROSINE. Not too well, Master Figaro. I'm dying of boredom.

FIGARO. I believe you. Only fools thrive on it.

ROSINE. Who were you talking to down there for so long? I didn't listen, but—

FIGARO. He's a young student, a relative of mine, and he shows great promise. He's witty, sensitive, talented, and he has a very nice face.   10

ROSINE. Oh, very attractive indeed, I must say. What's his name?

FIGARO. Lindor. He has nothing at all, but if he hadn't left Madrid in such a hurry he might have made something of himself there.

ROSINE. (*Impulsively*) He'll find something, Master Figaro, he'll find something. The man you describe was not created to remain obscure.

FIGARO. (*Aside*) Very good. (*Aloud*) But he has one serious fault that stands in his way.   20

ROSINE. A fault, Master Figaro, a fault? Are you sure?

FIGARO. He's in love.

ROSINE. In love! And you call that a fault?

FIGARO. Of course it's only a fault with regard to his poor prospects.

ROSINE. Oh, how unjust fate is! Has he told you the name of the person he loves? I'm so curious—

FIGARO. Oh, my lady, you're the last person I'd want to share a confidence like that with.   30

ROSINE. (*Sharply*) Why, Master Figaro? I'm discreet. I'm very much interested in this young relative of yours, so tell me—

FIGARO. (*With a sly look*) Imagine the prettiest little darling, sweet, tender, gentle, so fresh you want to eat her up; nimble feet, supple waist, slender, with round arms, a rosy mouth, and such hands! such cheeks! such teeth! such eyes!

ROSINE. Does she live in this city?

40   FIGARO. In this neighborhood.

ROSINE. In this street, maybe?

FIGARO. Two steps away from me.

ROSINE. Oh, how delightful—for your relative. And this person is—

FIGARO. Didn't I tell you her name?

ROSINE. (*Sharply*) It's the only thing you forgot, Master Figaro. Tell me, tell me quickly. If anyone comes in, I might never know—

FIGARO. You're sure you want to know, my lady?

50   Well then, this person is—your guardian's ward.

ROSINE. A ward?

FIGARO. —of Doctor Bartholo, yes, my lady.

ROSINE. (*Much moved*) Oh, Master Figaro, I don't believe you at all!

FIGARO. He's dying to convince you of it himself.

ROSINE. You make me tremble, Master Figaro.

FIGARO. Tremble, indeed! That's a bad policy, my lady. When you're afraid you might suffer, you're already suffering from fear. Besides, I'm here to put all

60   your guards out of the way until tomorrow.

ROSINE. If he loves me, he must prove it by keeping absolutely still.

FIGARO. Oh, my lady, how can love and repose live side by side in the same heart? Nowadays a poor youth, unfortunately, must make a terrible choice between love without repose, or repose without love.

ROSINE. (*Lowering her eyes*) Repose without love
—must be—

FIGARO. —pretty tiresome. It seems to me that love
without repose looks a little more attractive. And as 70
far as I am concerned, if I were a woman—

ROSINE. (*Embarrassed*) It's certainly impossible for
any young lady to prevent a good man from admiring
her.

FIGARO. As my relative admires you, to distraction.

ROSINE. But if he does anything indiscreet, Master
Figaro, he'll ruin us.

FIGARO. (*Aside*) Ruin *us!* (*Aloud*) If you were to
give him a particular warning in a little letter— Letters are very convincing.   80

ROSINE. (*Giving him the letter she just wrote*) I
haven't time to write this over again, but when you
give it to him—tell him—be sure to tell him—(*She
stops to listen.*)

FIGARO. No one is coming, my lady.

ROSINE. —that all I'm doing is purely out of friendship.

FIGARO. That's obvious. Good lord! Love is altogether different!

ROSINE. Pure friendship, you understand. I'm only
afraid that he might be discouraged by the difficul- 90
ties—

FIGARO. He might be if he were some fly-by-night.
But remember, my lady, the wind that puts out a candle sets the torch aflame, and we have a torch on our
hands. When he merely speaks of his love, he breathes

such fire that I almost burn with his passion, and I'm only a bystander.

ROSINE. Heavens! I hear my guardian! If he finds you here—! Go through the music room and down-
100 stairs as quietly as you can.

FIGARO. Don't worry. (*Aside, indicating the letter*) He'll like this better than anything I found out. (*He goes into the music room and hides there.*)

ROSINE. (*Alone*) I'll die of fright before he's out-side. How nice that good Figaro is; such an honest man, and so kind to his relatives. Oh, there's my jailer; I'd better get back to work.

(*She blows out the candle and sits down at an em-broidery frame. BARTHOLO enters angrily.*)

BARTHOLO. Oh, curses on that scoundrel, that pirate Figaro! There you are! You can't step out of the house for a single minute without being sure that when you
110 return—

ROSINE. Sir, who has made you so angry?

BARTHOLO. That damned barber. He's just crippled my whole household with one twist of the wrist. He gives a drug to Bright-Eyes, sneezing powder to The Boy, he bleeds Marceline's foot—even down to my poor mule; on the poor blind beast's eyes, a poultice! Just because he owes me a hundred écus he's doing his best to run up big bills. Just let him produce them! And nobody's in the hallway! You can walk into this
120 room as easily as the parade ground!

ROSINE. But who would come here besides yourself, sir?

BARTHOLO. I would rather suffer from groundless fears than take risks for lack of due precaution. There are bold and daring men everywhere— Wasn't there one just this morning, who cleverly picked up your song while I went down to get it? Oh, I—

ROSINE. You make something out of every trifle, just for the fun of it. The wind could easily have picked up the paper, or any passer-by, or anything 130 at all.

BARTHOLO. A wind! A passer-by! There is never a wind, madame, and never a passer-by in this world; but there is always someone there just for the purpose of picking up the papers that a woman pretends to drop by mistake.

ROSINE. Pretends, sir?

BARTHOLO. Yes, madame, pretends.

ROSINE. (*Aside*) Oh, what a wicked old man!

BARTHOLO. But it won't happen again; I'm going to 140 have that shutter nailed down.

ROSINE. Why stop there? Wall up the windows altogether! There's little difference between a prison and a dungeon.

BARTHOLO. For the windows on the street, that's not a bad idea. At least, I hope that barber wasn't here?

ROSINE. Are you jealous of him too?

BARTHOLO. As much as of anyone else.

ROSINE. How sweet you are to me!

BARTHOLO. Oh, if you trust everybody, you'll soon 150 have in your house a wife who's clever at deceit, good friends to carry her off, and good servants to help them.

ROSINE. What! You don't even trust me to resist Master Figaro?

BARTHOLO. Who the devil understands anything about a woman's quirks? And when have I ever seen any of your lofty principles—?

ROSINE. (*Angrily*) Well, sir, if women are pleased 160 by any man at all, why is it that you revolt me?

BARTHOLO. (*Stupefied*) What's that? What's that? Aren't you going to answer my question about the barber?

ROSINE. (*Outraged*) All right then! Yes, that man came here; I saw him; I talked to him. I won't even conceal the fact that I found him very pleasant. And now I hope you die of vexation! (*She goes out.*)

BARTHOLO. (*Alone*) Oh, those rascals! Those dogs of servants! Boy! Bright-Eyes! You no-good Bright- 170 Eyes!

(BRIGHT-EYES *enters, yawning and half asleep.*)

BRIGHT-EYES. Aah, aah, ah, ah—

BARTHOLO. Where were you, you infernal pest, when the barber was here?

BRIGHT-EYES. Sir, I was—aah, ah, ah—

BARTHOLO. Cooking up some mischief, no doubt. Didn't you see him?

BRIGHT-EYES. Sure I saw him, and he found I was very sick. That's what he said, and it must be true, because I began to feel pains all over, just listening to 180 him talk—aah, aah—

BARTHOLO. (*Imitating him*) Just listening to him! Where is that good-for-nothing Boy? Drugging this

poor child without a prescription from me! There's
something back of all this.

(*The* Boy *enters. He is an old man who walks with
a crutch and sneezes constantly.*)

BRIGHT-EYES. (*Still yawning*) Boy?

BARTHOLO. You can sneeze on Sunday.

BOY. That's more than fifty—fifty times—in a minute. (*He sneezes.*) I'm blown to bits.

BARTHOLO. Now! I asked both of you whether anyone entered Rosine's room, and you didn't tell me that   190
the barber—

BRIGHT-EYES. (*Still yawning*) Is Master Figaro somebody? Aah, aah—

BARTHOLO. I'll bet this rascal has an understanding
with him.

BRIGHT-EYES. (*Weeping idiotically*) Me? An understanding?

BOY. (*Sneezing*) But, sir, isn't there—isn't there any
justice?

BARTHOLO. Justice! That's all right between you two   200
wretches. But I'm your master, so I'm always right.

BOY. (*Sneezing*) But, gee, when something's true—

BARTHOLO. When something's true! If I don't want
it to be true, I'll see to it that it's not true. If we per-
mitted rascals like you to be right, what would become
of authority?

BOY. (*Sneezing*) I wish I could get fired. It's a bum
job, and a devil of a row going on all the time.

BRIGHT-EYES. (*Weeping*) A good decent man is
treated like a criminal.   210

BARTHOLO. Get out then, you poor decent man. (*He imitates them.*) Atchoo! Aah! One sneezes and the other yawns, right in my face!

BOY. Oh, sir, I swear if it wasn't for the young lady, there'd be—there'd be no staying in this house.

(*The servants go out, still sneezing and yawning.*)

BARTHOLO. What a state Figaro has put them in! I see what he's up to: the rascal wants to pay me my hundred écus without opening his purse.

(DON BAZILE *enters.* FIGARO, *hiding in the music room, is seen from time to time as he listens.*)

Oh, Don Bazile! Have you come to give Rosine her
220 music lesson?

BAZILE. That's the least of my concerns.

BARTHOLO. When I went to your house, I didn't find you.

BAZILE. I was attending to your affairs. I have some pretty bad news.

BARTHOLO. Bad for you?

BAZILE. No, for you. Count Almaviva is in town.

BARTHOLO. Not so loud! That man who searched for Rosine all over Madrid?

230 BAZILE. He's staying at a house near the market-place, and he goes out every day, in disguise.

BARTHOLO. Of course he's after us. What shall we do?

BAZILE. If he were an ordinary man, we could do away with him.

BARTHOLO. Yes, in a night ambush, with sword and buckler—

BAZILE. *Bone Deus!* And compromise ourselves? Stir up some mischief, that's more like it, and while it's working, we'll circulate some expert slanders, *concedo.* 240

BARTHOLO. That's an odd way to get rid of a man.

BAZILE. You have no respect for slander, sir? You don't know what you're talking about. I've seen it all but crush the best of men. Believe me, there's no downright evil, no horror, no absurdity that the idlers of a big city won't take if you go about it the right way, and we have some real experts at it here. It begins with a gentle whisper, skimming the earth like a swallow before the storm, *pianissimo,* it murmurs and twists and leaves its trail of poison. Whoever picks it 250 up, *piano, piano,* he slips it smoothly into your ear. The lie is planted, it sprouts, it grows, it moves, and *rinforzando,* it goes like the devil from one mouth to the next; then suddenly, I don't know how, you see slander rising, hissing, swelling, and growing before your eyes. It rushes out, extends its wings, spins, envelops, tears, bursts, and thunders, and becomes, by the grace of heaven, a general cry, a public *crescendo,* a universal chorus of hate and denunciation. Who the devil could withstand it? 260

BARTHOLO. What kind of nonsense are you talking, Bazile? And what has this *piano-crescendo* to do with my problem?

BAZILE. What has it to do with you? What everybody does to get rid of enemies, we must do to keep yours from getting any closer.

BARTHOLO. Closer! I'm going to marry Rosine before she even knows this Count exists.

BAZILE. In that case, you have no time to lose.

270   BARTHOLO. Who's delaying? You have charge of all the details in this affair.

BAZILE. Yes, but you've skimped on the expenses. In the harmony of a well-ordered society, an unequal marriage, a crooked verdict, an obvious injustice are discords which should always be prepared and resolved by the perfect concord of gold.

BARTHOLO. (*Giving him money*) All right, you must have it your way. But let's get on with it.

BAZILE. That's the way to talk. Tomorrow every-
280 thing will be over. You must be careful to see that no one warns your ward today.

BARTHOLO. Trust me. Are you coming this evening, Bazile?

BAZILE. Don't count on it. Your marriage alone will keep me busy all day. Don't count on it.

BARTHOLO. (*Going to the door with him*) Your servant.

BAZILE. Don't bother, doctor; don't go downstairs.

BARTHOLO. Oh, yes. I want to close the street door
290 after you.

(*They go out.* FIGARO *enters from the music room.*)

FIGARO. Now, there's a wise precaution. By all means close the street door, and I'll open it for the Count when I go. What a rogue that Bazile is! Fortunately, his stupidity is even greater. You need position, family, name, rank—in short, something to go on—if you're going to get anywhere in the world as a slanderer. But a Bazile! Nobody believes his lies!

(ROSINE *runs in.*)

ROSINE. What! Are you still here, Master Figaro?

FIGARO. Lucky for you, my lady. Your guardian and your singing teacher thought they were alone, and they've told me everything that's on their minds.

ROSINE. Did you listen to them, Master Figaro? Don't you know that's very wrong?

FIGARO. Listening? That's the best way to hear anything. Now I know that your guardian plans to marry you tomorrow.

ROSINE. Oh, good heavens!

FIGARO. Don't be afraid. We'll keep him so busy he won't have time to think about it.

ROSINE. He's coming back. Go down the back stairs. You're scaring me to death.

(FIGARO *runs off, and* BARTHOLO *enters.*)

Was someone here to see you, sir?

BARTHOLO. Don Bazile, whom I showed out the door, and with good reason. Would you prefer that it was Master Figaro?

ROSINE. It makes no difference to me, I assure you.

BARTHOLO. I'd like to know what that barber was so anxious to tell you.

ROSINE. Would you really like to know? He brought me a report on Marceline's health, which is none too good, according to him.

BARTHOLO. A report! I'll bet he was commissioned to bring you a letter.

ROSINE. From whom, if you please?

BARTHOLO. Oh, from whom! From someone women never name. How should I know? Perhaps an answer to that paper you dropped from the window.

ROSINE. (*Aside*) He never misses a thing! (*Aloud*) It would serve you right if it were!

330   BARTHOLO. (*Examining her hands*) It was. You've been writing.

ROSINE. (*Embarrassed*) I suppose you'd enjoy trying to make me admit it.

BARTHOLO. (*Taking her right hand*) Oh, not at all. But there's still a spot of ink on your finger. How about that, sly señora?

ROSINE. (*Aside*) What a disgusting man!

BARTHOLO. (*Still holding her hand*) A woman thinks she's safe whenever she's alone.

340   ROSINE. Oh, no doubt that's a sure proof! Stop, sir, you're twisting my arm. I burned my finger while I was sewing near the candle, and they say you should put ink on it right away. That's what I did.

BARTHOLO. That's what you did? Then let's see if a second witness confirms the testimony of the first. I'm sure there are six sheets of paper in this packet because I count them every morning, including this one.

ROSINE. (*Aside*) Oh, how foolish of me!

BARTHOLO. (*Counting*) Three, four, five—

350   ROSINE. The sixth—

BARTHOLO. I see quite clearly that there is no sixth.

ROSINE. (*Lowering her eyes*) The sixth—I used to

make a cone for some candy I sent to the little Figaro girl.

BARTHOLO. The little Figaro girl. And the pen was a new one—why is it now black? Was it from writing the address of the little Figaro girl?

ROSINE. (*Aside*) This man is jealous by instinct. (*Aloud*) I used it to draw over the lines of a flower that rubbed off the jacket I'm embroidering.

BARTHOLO. How edifying! If you expect me to believe you, my child, you mustn't blush while you go on and on varnishing the truth like that. But you haven't much experience yet.

ROSINE. Well, who wouldn't blush, sir, to hear such horrid deductions drawn from the most innocent facts?

BARTHOLO. Of course, I'm wrong. To burn a finger and dip it in the ink, to make cones for candy for the little Figaro girl, and to draw embroidery designs on a jacket! What could be more innocent? And what a heap of lies to conceal a single fact! "I'm alone, no one's watching me, I can tell whatever stories I please." But the end of the finger remains black, the pen is soiled, the paper missing! You can't think of everything. You may be sure, señora, when I go into town, a double turn of the key will answer to me for you.

(*The* COUNT *enters, in a cavalry uniform, pretending to be drunk, and singing, "Let's wake her."*)

What does this fellow want with us? A soldier! Go to your room, señora.

(*The* COUNT, *still singing, advances toward* ROSINE.)

380   COUNT. Which of you two ladies is named Doctor Balordo? (*Aside to* ROSINE) I am Lindor.

    BARTHOLO. Bartholo!

    ROSINE. (*Aside*) He said Lindor!

    COUNT. Balordo, Barque-à-l'eau—that's a pretty good name. But the question is, which one of you— (*To* ROSINE, *showing her a paper*) Take this letter.

    BARTHOLO. Which one! You can see very well that I am! Which one, indeed! Go to your room, Rosine. This man must be drunk.

390   ROSINE. That's why I'd better stay, sir. You're alone, and a woman sometimes inspires a little respect.

    BARTHOLO. Go on, go on. I'm not afraid.

(ROSINE *goes off.*)

    COUNT. Oh, I recognized you right away, from your description. (*He puts away the letter.*)

    BARTHOLO. What's that you're hiding in your pocket?

    COUNT. It's something I'm hiding so you won't know what it is.

    BARTHOLO. My description! These people always think they're talking to soldiers.

400   COUNT. Do you think you're hard to describe? (*He sings.*)

> A nodding pate, hair like a mop,
> Except where it is bald on top,
> Two eyes at odds, and looking wild,
> Manners worse than sulky child,
> A figure heavy as a lump,
> One shoulder with a little slump,
> Skin as tough as ancient leather,

Nose like a shelter from the weather,
A leg that's fat and rather bent,
A voice that's hardly eloquent,   410
Appetites out of all control—
A doctor to his very soul.

BARTHOLO. What do you mean? Did you come here to insult me? Get out of here! At once!

COUNT. Get out! That's not a nice way to speak. Do you know how to read, Doctor—Barbe-à-l'eau?

BARTHOLO. Another silly question.

COUNT. Oh, you needn't be ashamed to admit that you can't. I can't either, and I'm at least as much of a doctor as you are.   420

BARTHOLO. What's that?

COUNT. I'm the regiment's horse-doctor. That's why they lodged me here, with a colleague.

BARTHOLO. Do they dare to compare a veterinary—

COUNT. (*Speaking*)
No, doctor, I will never claim
Our art to have so great a fame
As Hippocrates and his crew.
                    (*Singing*)
All the praise belongs to you,
My comrade, for your greater skill:
When you can't remove the ill,   430
You rub out the patient too.

Isn't it polite of me to speak this way?

BARTHOLO. You ignorant artisan, it's not becoming for you to revile the first, the greatest, the most useful of the arts.

COUNT. Very useful to those who practice it.

BARTHOLO. The very sun glories in shining on its triumphs.

COUNT. And the earth hastens to cover its mistakes.

440 BARTHOLO. You flippant ignoramus! It's obvious you're accustomed to speak only to horses.

COUNT. Speak to horses? Oh, doctor, not very clever! Doesn't everybody know that the veterinary always cures his patients without a word, while on the other hand the doctor never stops talking to his?

BARTHOLO. Without curing them, I suppose?

COUNT. You said it yourself.

BARTHOLO. Who the devil sent this blasted drunkard here?

450 COUNT. I think you're shooting epigrams at me, little Cupid!

BARTHOLO. Well, what do you want? What are you here for?

COUNT. (*Pretending to be angry*) Oh, so you're getting rough! What do I want? Can't you see?

(ROSINE *runs in.*)

ROSINE. Mister soldier, don't be angry, please. (*To* BARTHOLO) Speak to him gently, sir. When a man's unreasonable—

COUNT. You're right; he is unreasonable. But we're 460 reasonable, we are. I'm witty, and you're pretty— that's enough. For that matter, I don't want to have anything to do with anybody in this house but you.

ROSINE. What can I do for you, Mister Soldier?

COUNT. The smallest trifle, my child. But if there's any obscurity in anything I say—

ROSINE. I'll catch the spirit of it.

COUNT. (*Showing her the letter*) No, stick to the letter, to the letter. It only concerns—your giving me a place to sleep tonight.

BARTHOLO. Is that all?   470

COUNT. That's all. Read the sweet little note our officer has written you.

BARTHOLO. Let me see it.

(*The* COUNT *hides the letter and gives another to* BARTHOLO, *which he reads.*)

"Doctor Bartholo is to receive, feed, lodge, and bed—"

COUNT. (*Reading over his shoulder*) Bed!

BARTHOLO. "—for one night only, the above-named Lindor, known as the scholar, a soldier of the regiment—"

ROSINE. It's he! The very man!

BARTHOLO. (*Quickly to* ROSINE) What's that?   480

COUNT. Well now, am I wrong, Doctor Barbaro?

BARTHOLO. This man seems to take a perverse pleasure in butchering my name in every way he can. Go to the devil with your Barbaro, Barbe-à-l'eau! And tell that impertinent officer that since my trip to Madrid I'm exempt from lodging military men.

COUNT. (*Aside*) Oh, heavens, what bad luck!

BARTHOLO. Ah, ha, my friend. That baffles you, and sobers you up a little! Now clear out of here right this minute.   490

COUNT. (*Aside*) I almost gave myself away. (*Aloud*) Clear out! Even if you're exempt from military men, I hope you're not exempt from being polite! Clear out!

Let's see your certificate of exemption. Even if I can't read, I'll soon see—

BARTHOLO. What difference does it make? It's in the bureau.

(*While he goes to get it, the* COUNT *speaks softly, without moving.*)

COUNT. Oh, my beautiful Rosine.

ROSINE. Are you really Lindor?

500   COUNT. Take this letter somehow.

ROSINE. Be careful; he's watching us.

COUNT. Take out your handkerchief and I'll drop it. (*He approaches her.*)

BARTHOLO. Take it easy, Mister Soldier. I don't like anyone too close to my wife.

COUNT. Is she your wife?

BARTHOLO. What if she is?

COUNT. I took you for her grandfather, paternal, maternal, sempiternal. There must be at least three generations between you and her.

510   BARTHOLO. (*Reading a parchment*) "In consideration of good and thoughtful services rendered to us—"

COUNT. (*Knocking the parchment out of his hands onto the floor*) What good are all these words!

BARTHOLO. Are you aware, soldier, that if I call my servants you'll get the treatment you deserve?

COUNT. A battle? Good, a battle! That's my trade. (*Patting the pistol in his belt*) I have something here to throw dust in their eyes. Have you ever watched a battle, madame?

ROSINE. Nor ever wished to.

COUNT. But nothing is as much fun as a battle! (*He* 520
pushes the doctor.) Now imagine in the first place the
enemy on one side of a ravine and our friends on the
other. (*To* ROSINE, *showing her the letter*) Take out
your handkerchief. (*He spits on the floor.*) There's the
ravine, you see.

(ROSINE *takes out the handkerchief and the* COUNT
drops the letter between them.)

BARTHOLO. (*Stooping for it*) Ah, ha!

COUNT (*Picking it up again*) Hold on! I was about
to let you in on the secrets of my trade. A very discreet wife, to be sure. Isn't that a love letter that fell
from her pocket?   530

BARTHOLO. Give it to me, give it to me.

COUNT. *Dulciter*, papa! Each to his own calling. It's
just as natural as if a prescription for rhubarb fell from
yours.

ROSINE. (*Reaching for the letter*) Oh, I know what
it is, Mister Soldier. (*She takes the letter and hides it
in the little pocket of her apron.*)

BARTHOLO. Now will you get out?

COUNT. All right, I'll go. Goodby, doctor, no hard
feelings. Wish me well, sweetheart. Ask death to let
me go for a few more campaigns. Life was never be- 540
fore so dear to me.

BARTHOLO. Never mind. If I had any credit with
death—

COUNT. Credit with death? Aren't you a doctor? You
do so much for him, he can't refuse you a favor in return.

(*He goes and* BARTHOLO *looks after him.*)

BARTHOLO. At last he's gone. (*Aside*) Now I'll lead her on.

ROSINE. You must admit he's merry, that young sol-
550 dier. Even though he's drunk, you can see he's not without wit, and some education.

BARTHOLO. Luckily, my dear, we managed to get rid of him. But aren't you eager to read me the paper he handed you?

ROSINE. What paper?

BARTHOLO. The one he got you to accept by pre-tending to pick it up for you.

ROSINE. Oh! That was the letter from my cousin, the officer, that fell out of my pocket.

560 BARTHOLO. I had an idea that he took it out of his own pocket.

ROSINE. I recognized it right away.

BARTHOLO. What must I do to have a look at it?

ROSINE. The only thing is, I don't know what I've done with it.

BARTHOLO. (*Indicating the pocket*) You put it there.

ROSINE. Oh, yes, without thinking.

BARTHOLO. Oh, of course. You'll find it's some fool-ishness.

570 ROSINE. (*Aside*) The only way to put him off is to make him angry.

BARTHOLO. Give it to me, my dear.

ROSINE. But what do you mean by insisting on it, sir? Do you still mistrust me?

BARTHOLO. But what do you mean by keeping it from me?

ROSINE. I tell you again, sir, it's only a letter from my cousin that you brought me yesterday, unsealed. And speaking of that, I tell you frankly that I'm much displeased by these liberties you take.   580

BARTHOLO. I don't understand you.

ROSINE. Do I go through every paper that comes for you? Why do you think you have a right to pry into everything that's addressed to me? If this is jealousy, it insults me; if it's an abuse of usurped power, I'm even more disgusted.

BARTHOLO. What, disgusted? You've never spoken to me like that before.

ROSINE. If I've been patient all this time, I didn't mean to give you a right to offend me with impunity. 590

BARTHOLO. What offense are you talking about?

ROSINE. It's unheard of to open other people's letters.

BARTHOLO. Even your wife's?

ROSINE. I'm not your wife yet. And why should a wife be singled out for an insult you wouldn't give anyone else?

BARTHOLO. You're trying to put me off and make me forget that letter, which must be a message from some lover. But I tell you I'm going to see it.   600

ROSINE. You're not going to see it. If you come near me, I'll run right out of the house and ask protection from the first person I meet.

BARTHOLO. You won't get it.

ROSINE. We'll see about that.

BARTHOLO. We aren't in France, where they always assume that a woman is right. But to keep you from trying it, I'm going to lock the door.

ROSINE. (*While he goes out to lock it*) Good heav-
610 ens, what shall I do? I'll exchange this letter for my cousin's and let him do whatever he likes with that. (*She exchanges the letters, putting the cousin's letter in her pocket so that it can be plainly seen.*)

BARTHOLO. (*Returning*) And now I expect to see it.

ROSINE. By what right, if you please?

BARTHOLO. By the universally recognized right of might.

ROSINE. You'll have to kill me first.

BARTHOLO. (*Stamping his foot*) Madame! Madame!

ROSINE. (*Falling into a chair and pretending to collapse*) Oh, what an outrage!

BARTHOLO. Give me that letter before I get angry.

620 ROSINE. (*Sinking back*) Oh, poor Rosine!

BARTHOLO. What's the matter with you?

ROSINE. What a frightful future!

BARTHOLO. Rosine!

ROSINE. I'm choking with rage.

BARTHOLO. She's ill.

ROSINE. I'm fainting. I'm dying.

BARTHOLO. (*Feeling her pulse, aside*) Good heavens, there's the letter. I can read it before she knows I have it. (*While feeling her pulse, he takes the letter and tries to read it by turning away from her.*)

630 ROSINE. (*Still collapsed*) Poor me! Ooh!

BARTHOLO. (*Putting down her arm, aside*) How mad

we are to learn what we fear to know.

ROSINE. Oh, poor Rosine!

BARTHOLO. The use of perfume—produces these spasmodic attacks. (*He reads behind her chair, while he feels her pulse.* ROSINE *rises a little, looks at him, nods, and falls back.* BARTHOLO *speaks aside.*) Good heavens! It's her cousin's letter! My blasted suspicions! Now how can I make up with her? At least I don't want her to know I read it. (*While pretending to support her, he slips the letter back into her pocket.*)

ROSINE. (*Sighing*) Ah! 640

BARTHOLO. Well now, it's nothing, my child. A slight attack of the vapors, that's all. Your pulse hasn't missed a single beat. (*He goes to the table for a flask.*)

ROSINE. (*Aside*) He put the letter back; very good.

BARTHOLO. My dear Rosine, try a little of these spirits.

ROSINE. I want nothing from you. Leave me alone.

BARTHOLO. I admit I was unreasonable about the letter.

ROSINE. Oh, it's not the letter. It's the way you ask 650 for things that's disgusting.

BARTHOLO. (*On his knees*) Pardon me. I realized my mistake very quickly. And now you see me at your feet, ready to make amends for it.

ROSINE. Why should I pardon you when you won't believe that this is my cousin's letter?

BARTHOLO. Whether it is or not, I don't want any explanation.

ROSINE. (*Offering him the letter*) You see? When

660 you behave nicely you can have anything you want. Read it.

BARTHOLO. Your frankness would dispel my suspicions if I were so unfortunate as to have any left.

ROSINE. Now read it, sir.

BARTHOLO. (*Drawing back*) God forbid that I should insult you in that way.

ROSINE. You'll offend me if you refuse.

BARTHOLO. Let me make amends by giving you this assurance of my perfect confidence in you. I'm going 670 up to see poor Marceline. Figaro bled her foot; I can't imagine why. Won't you come too?

ROSINE. I'll come up in a minute.

BARTHOLO. Now that we've made peace, my darling, give me your hand. If only you could love me, how happy you could be.

ROSINE. (*Lowering her eyes*) If only you could make me happy, oh, how I would love you!

BARTHOLO. I'll make you happy! I'll make you happy! I give you my word that I'll make you happy! (*He goes out.*)

680 ROSINE. (*Watching him go*) Oh, Lindor! He says he'll make me happy! Now I must read this letter that almost caused me so much trouble. (*She reads and exclaims:*) Oh! I've read it too late! He wants me to start an open quarrel with my guardian. I just had a good opportunity, and I let it go. When I received the letter I felt my self blush all the way up to my eyes. Oh, my guardian is right. I have none of those worldly manners that he often tells me women use to keep

their composure under any circumstances. But an unjust man would make a schemer out of innocence it-   690
self!

Act III

BARTHOLO. (*Brooding miserably, alone*) What a temper! What a temper! But she did seem to get over it. I wish somebody would tell me who the devil put the idea into her head that she doesn't want any more lessons from Don Bazile! She must know that he's got something to do with the wedding . . .

(*There is a knock at the door.*)

You can do everything in the world to please a woman, and then if you leave out just one little thing—just one—

(*Another knock at the door*)

10 Let's see who that is.

(*The* COUNT *enters, dressed as a student.*)

COUNT. May peace and joy forever abide herein!

BARTHOLO. (*Shortly*) Never came a wish more timely. What do you want?

COUNT. Sir, I am Alonzo, a student, a licensed tutor—

BARTHOLO. I don't need a tutor.

COUNT. —pupil of Don Bazile, organist at the con-

46

vent, who has the honor to teach music to Madame your—

BARTHOLO. Bazile! Organist! Who has the honor! 20 I know all that! Perfectly!

COUNT. (*Aside*) What a man! (*Aloud*) A sudden illness has kept him in bed—

BARTHOLO. In bed! Bazile? I'm glad he sent you. I'll go to see him this minute.

COUNT. (*Aside*) Oh, the devil! (*Aloud*) When I say in bed, sir, I mean—in his room.

BARTHOLO. Even if it's only a slight illness. Go ahead; I'll follow you.

COUNT. (*Embarrassed*) Sir, I was sent—Can any- 30 one hear us?

BARTHOLO. (*Aside*) This must be some trick. (*Aloud*) Oh, no, mystery man. Speak without any more fuss, if you can.

COUNT. (*Aside*) Blasted old man! (*Aloud*) Don Bazile sent me to tell you—

BARTHOLO. Speak louder. I'm deaf in one ear.

COUNT. Oh, certainly. (*He raises his voice.*)—that Count Almaviva, who was staying near the market-place— 40

BARTHOLO. (*Frightened*) Speak softer, speak softer.

COUNT. (*Louder*)—left there this morning. Since it was through me that he knew that Count Almaviva—

BARTHOLO. Softer! Speak softer, please!

COUNT. (*Still loud*)—was in the city, and since I discovered that Señora Rosine wrote to him—

BARTHOLO. Wrote to him? My good friend, not so loud, I beg you. Now let's sit down and have a friendly chat. You discovered, you say, that Rosine—

50   COUNT. (*Arrogantly*) Certainly. Bazile was disturbed about this correspondence on your account, and he asked me to show you her letter. But the way you take things—

BARTHOLO. Oh, for heaven's sake, I take things well. But can't you speak any more softly?

COUNT. You told me you're deaf in one ear.

BARTHOLO. I'm sorry, Mister Alonzo, if you found me suspicious and harsh. I'm utterly surrounded by plotters and ambushes. Besides, your appearance,
60 your age, your manner—Pardon me. Well then, you have the letter?

COUNT. In a minute. If you behave this way, sir— But I'm afraid someone might hear.

BARTHOLO. Oh, who could hear us? All my servants are under the weather. Rosine has shut herself up in a rage. The devil is loose in my house. But I'm going to make sure—(*He opens* ROSINE's *door quietly.*)

COUNT. (*Aside*) I've put my foot in it by being too hasty. Shall I keep the letter for now? Then I'd have to
70 leave, and I might as well not have come. Show him the letter? If I can warn Rosine, it would be a masterstroke to show it to him.

BARTHOLO. (*Returning on tiptoe*) She's sitting near the window with her back to the door, busily reading over a letter from her cousin the officer that I opened. Now let's see hers.

COUNT. (*Giving him* ROSINE's *letter*) Here it is. (*Aside*) That's my letter she's reading.

BARTHOLO. (*Reading*) "Since you told me your

name and rank—" Oh, the little sneak! That's her 80 handwriting all right!

COUNT. (*Frightened*) Now it's your turn to speak softer.

BARTHOLO. I'm greatly obliged to you, my friend.

COUNT. If you feel that you owe me anything for it, when all this is over, you won't any longer. After a certain business Don Bazile is now arranging with a lawyer—

BARTHOLO. With a lawyer, about my wedding?

COUNT. Isn't that just what I mean? He asked me to 90 tell you that everything may be ready tomorrow. Then, if she resists—

BARTHOLO. She will resist.

COUNT. (*Trying to take back the letter, which* BARTHOLO *retains*) That's when I can help you. We'll show her the letter, and, if necessary—(*More mysteriously*)—I'll go so far as to say that I got it from a woman the Count gave it to. Then you see, her anxiety, shame, and spite may lead her right away—

BARTHOLO. (*Laughing*) Slander! My good friend, now I'm sure Bazile sent you. But this may look pre- 100 arranged unless she meets you beforehand.

COUNT. (*Hiding a start of joy*) Don Bazile thought so too. But how can we manage it? It's late—not much time left—

BARTHOLO. I'll say you came in his place. Won't you give her a lesson?

COUNT. There's nothing I won't do to please you. But remember that these stories of substitute teachers are old tricks in all the comedies. If she suspects—

110 BARTHOLO. When I introduce you, how could she? You look more like a lover in disguise than an accomplice.

COUNT. I do? You think my manner will help to fool her?

BARTHOLO. It would take a sharp eye to see through you. She's in a bad mood this evening. If she'll only meet you—Her harpsichord is over here. Amuse yourself while you're waiting. I'm going to do the impossible and get her in here.

120 COUNT. Be sure not to mention the letter.

BARTHOLO. Not before the right moment! That would ruin the whole effect. You don't have to tell me a thing twice. I don't have to be told a second time. (*He goes.*)

COUNT. I'm saved! Ugh! This devil of a man is hard to manage. Figaro was right about him. I could see myself when I told those lies. I looked silly and awkward, and he has eyes in his head. My word, if I hadn't had that sudden inspiration about the letter, I

130 must admit I would have gone on like a fool. Oh, heavens, they're arguing in there. What if she's too stubborn to come out? I'd better listen. She's refusing to leave her room, and I've lost all the advantage I gained by this trick. (*He listens again.*) Here she comes! I'd better not be seen right away.

(*He goes into the music room,* ROSINE *and* BARTHOLO *enter.*)

ROSINE. (*Pretending to be angry*) Whatever you're

going to say is useless, sir. I've made up my mind. I dont want to hear anything more about music.

BARTHOLO. Listen, my child. This is Mister Alonzo, Don Bazile's friend and pupil. He's chosen him to be 140 one of our witnesses. Music will calm you, I assure you.

ROSINE. Oh, there's no chance of that. Me sing this evening! Where is this teacher you're so afraid to send away? I'll settle his business and Bazile's too, in two words. (*She sees her lover and cries out.*) Oh!

BARTHOLO. What's the matter?

ROSINE. (*Clasping her hands over her heart in distress*) Oh, good heavens, sir! Oh, good heavens, sir!

BARTHOLO. She's ill again, Mister Alonzo.

ROSINE. No, I'm not ill—but, when I turned—oh! 150

COUNT. You turned your ankle, madame?

ROSINE. Oh, yes, I turned my ankle. It hurt very badly.

COUNT. I could see that it did.

ROSINE. (*Gazing at the* COUNT) It struck me to the heart.

BARTHOLO. Sit down, sit down. Isn't there a chair here? (*He goes to find one.*)

COUNT. Ah, Rosine!

ROSINE. What a chance you're taking!   160

COUNT. I have a thousand important things to tell you.

ROSINE. He won't leave us alone.

COUNT. Figaro is coming to help us.

BARTHOLO. (*Carrying a chair*) There, my darling,

sit down. It's out of the question, mister tutor, for her to take a lesson this evening. It must wait till another day. Goodby.

ROSINE. (*To the* COUNT) No, wait. I feel a little
170 better now. (*To* BARTHOLO) I'm afraid I wronged you, sir, and I want to do as you did, to make amends immediately—

BARTHOLO. Oh, what good little natures women have! But after an experience like that, my child, I can't allow you to exert yourself in the least. Goodby, goodby, tutor.

ROSINE. (*To the* COUNT) Just a moment please! (*To* BARTHOLO) You'll lead me to think, sir, that you're unwilling to oblige me unless you permit me to show
180 my regret by taking my lesson.

COUNT. (*Aside, to* BARTHOLO) Don't cross her, if you want my advice.

BARTHOLO. That's enough, my sweet. I'm so far from wishing to displease you that I'll stay here through your entire lesson.

ROSINE. No, sir. I know that music doesn't appeal to you.

BARTHOLO. I assure you that I'll be enchanted this evening.

190 ROSINE. (*Aside to the* COUNT) This is torture.

COUNT. (*Taking a piece of music from the stand*) Is this what you wish to sing, Madame?

ROSINE. Oh, yes. It's a pretty little piece from *The Useless Precaution.*

BARTHOLO. There's that *Useless Precaution* again!

COUNT. It's the very latest thing. It describes spring

in a lively style. Does Madame wish to try it?

ROSINE. (*Gazing at the* COUNT) With great pleasure.
A picture of spring is enchanting. It's nature's youth.
When we emerge from winter, the heart seems to
feel a greater degree of sensibility, just as a slave who
has been long confined enjoys liberty all the more   200
when it's given to him.

BARTHOLO. (*Aside to the* COUNT) Her head's always full of these romantic ideas.

COUNT. (*Aside to* BARTHOLO) Do you see her point?

BARTHOLO. My word! (*He sits in the chair* ROSINE
had occupied, while she sings.)

ROSINE.

> When on the plain
> Love brings again
>   Happy spring,
> The lovers sing.
> All comes to life,   210
> And, sharp as knife,
>   Every flower
> And heart can feel its power.
> Out under the sky
> Come the flocks young and spry;
> Their spirits soar high;
> Young lambs give a cry,
>   So gay and bold,
>   Out from the fold,
>   Joy they know,   220
>   Strong they grow.
> The ewes graze on
> New flowers that blazon

The grass, and nearby
The dog's watchful eye.
But Lindor, all aglow,
Dreams only this:
With his shepherdess to know
Love's sweet bliss.
230   Lonely, this miss,
Seeking his kiss,
Goes with a song
Where her lover waits so long.
Love is quick
To play a trick;
Will he suspect
That song has great effect?
Those sweet rustic pipes,
The birds of all types,
240   The sounds in her ears,
Her fresh sixteen years,
All invite her
And excite her
Set a-swirl
The heart of a girl.
From Lindor's bower
He spies this flower;
First he meets her,
Then he greets her
250   With a soft and clinging kiss.
She finds it sweet,
But tells him it is all amiss,
So he'll entreat.
All the treasures,

The promises and pains,
   All the pleasures,
The joys and cares—
All these are theirs.
When love overrules,
Her anger cools.   260
If any prying eye
Upon this scene should seek to spy,
   The lovers both agree
To take great care . . .
That none their love may see.
   For when they dare
To flout Fate's harsh decree,
   Their love's more rare.

(BARTHOLO *falls asleep while he listens. During the
last verse, the* COUNT *ventures to take her hand and
cover it with kisses. Her emotion causes* ROSINE *to
sing slower and softer, until, four lines from the end,
at the word* care, *she stops altogether, and the orchestra stops with her.* BARTHOLO *is awakened by the ab-
sence of the sound that put him to sleep. The* COUNT
rises, and ROSINE *and the orchestra quickly finish the
song. If the last verse is encored, the same business is
played again.*)

COUNT. It's a charming song, to be sure, and Madame does it with so much understanding—   270
ROSINE. You flatter me, sir. All the credit belongs to
the teacher.
BARTHOLO. (*Yawning*) Well, I do believe I slept a

little during that delightful song. I have my weak-
nesses. I'm always coming and going and running in
circles, and as soon as I sit down, my poor legs—
(*He gets up and pushes the chair away.*)

ROSINE. (*Aside, to the* COUNT) Figaro isn't here yet.

COUNT. We'll have to kill some time.

BARTHOLO. But tell me, tutor—I've already asked
280 Bazile—isn't there any way to make her study something gayer than all these grand arias that go up and
down and rolling along—hi, ho, a, a, a, a,—they remind
me of a funeral. Something like those little airs we
all sang when I was young—they were so easy to remember. I used to know some. Here's one.

(*During the introduction to the music he scratches
his head; then, while he sings, he snaps his fingers
and dances with the bent knees of an old man.*)

> Here you are, my Rosinette,
>   You can get
> A husband who's a prize—

(*To the* COUNT, *laughing*) It's Fanchonette in the
290 song, but I changed it to Rosinette to please her, and
to make it fit the case. Ha, ha, ha! Pretty good, isn't it?

COUNT. (*Laughing*) Ha, ha, ha! Yes, all the better!

(FIGARO *enters and remains at the back.*)

BARTHOLO.
> Here you are, my Rosinette,
>   You can get
> A husband who's a prize.
> No Adonis in your eyes,

But at night, in the dark,
  I still know my way;
    And there, we remark,
The best of cats are gray.   300

(*He repeats the second part.* FIGARO, *behind him, mimics him.*)

No Adonis in your eyes, etc.
(*He sees* FIGARO.) Oh, come in, mister barber, come in! How nice you look!

FIGARO. (*Saluting him*) Well, sir, it's true that my mother used to tell me that, but I've declined somewhat since then. (*Aside, to the* COUNT) Good work, sir.

(*Throughout the following scene, the* COUNT *tries to speak to* ROSINE, *but the restless and vigilant eye of her guardian always prevents him. This makes a continuous pantomime for the actors not engaged in the dialogue between the* DOCTOR *and* FIGARO.)

BARTHOLO. Have you come back with more purgings, and bleedings, and druggings to put my entire household to bed again?   310

FIGARO. Oh, no. You can't have that much fun every day. But you know now that I'm not limited to routine attentions; when I'm really needed my zeal doesn't wait for orders—

BARTHOLO. Your zeal doesn't wait! Well, Mister Zeal, what have you to say to that poor wretch who yawns and sleeps when he's wide awake? And to that other one who has sneezed enough in the past three

hours to crack his skull and blow his brains out?
320 What have you to say to them?

FIGARO. What have I to say to them?

BARTHOLO. Yes.

FIGARO. I'll say to them—Oh, well, to the one who
sneezes I'll say, "God bless you," and "Go to bed" to
the one who yawns. And I won't charge you extra for
that either, sir.

BARTHOLO. I should hope not. But the bleedings
and the medicines will go onto the bill, if I let you get
away with it. Was it zeal that made you tie up my
330 mule's eyes? Will your poultice restore his sight?

FIGARO. Well, if it won't restore his sight, at least it
won't stop him from seeing.

BARTHOLO. Just let me find it on the bill! I never
heard of such extravagance.

FIGARO. My word, sir, the only choice we poor men
have is between stupidity and folly. So, where I can't
see any profit, at least I want to have some fun—hur-
rah for joy! Who knows whether the world will last
another three weeks?

340   BARTHOLO. Mister logician, you'd be better off to
pay me my hundred écus, and the interest, without
any more nonsense. I'm warning you.

FIGARO. Do you doubt my honesty, sir? Your hundred écus! I'd rather owe them to you all my life than
deny the debt for a single moment.

BARTHOLO. And tell me how your little girl liked the
candy you took her this morning.

FIGARO. What candy? What do you mean?

BARTHOLO. You know, that candy in a cone made of letter-paper—this morning. 350

FIGARO. Devil take me if—

ROSINE. (*Interrupting*) You didn't forget to give it to her for me, did you, Master Figaro? I asked you to.

FIGARO. Oh, oh! That candy this morning! How stupid of me! I'd completely lost track of that. Oh, it was fine, Madame, excellent!

BARTHOLO. Fine! Excellent! Yes, no doubt, mister barber. Now you're backtracking. You're playing a fine game, sir—

FIGARO. What's the matter with it, sir? 360

BARTHOLO. It will give you a fine reputation, sir.

FIGARO. I'll live up to it, sir.

BARTHOLO. Better say you'll live it down, sir.

FIGARO. As you like, sir.

BARTHOLO. You're taking a high tone, sir. I'll have you know that when I argue with an ass I never give in to him.

FIGARO. (*Turning his back*) That's where we differ, sir. I always give in to one.

BARTHOLO. What's that? What does he mean by that, 370 tutor?

FIGARO. I mean that you think you're dealing with some village barber who can't handle anything but his razor. I'll have you know, sir, that I used to wield a pen in Madrid, and if it weren't for the envious people—

BARTHOLO. Then why didn't you stay there, instead of coming here and changing your profession?

FIGARO. We do what we can. Put yourself in my
380 place.

BARTHOLO. Put myself in your place! Ye gods, I'd
say some pretty stupid things.

FIGARO. You're off to a pretty good start, sir. I'm
sure your colleague thinks so, who's dreaming over
there—

COUNT. (*Coming to himself*) I—I'm not his colleague.

FIGARO. You're not? When I saw you here in consultation, I thought you had some pursuit in common.

390   BARTHOLO. (*Angrily*) Well, what do you want here
anyway? Have you another letter to deliver to Madame this evening? Tell me! Shall I leave you alone?

FIGARO. You're so hard on the poor world! My word,
sir, I only came to shave you, that's all. Isn't this your
day?

BARTHOLO. You can come back later.

FIGARO. Oh, sure, come back later! Tomorrow morning the entire garrison gets medicine; it took a lot of
pull to swing the contract for me. How much time do
400 you think I have to waste? Will the gentleman come
to his room?

BARTHOLO. No, the gentleman will not come to his
room. But—why can't you shave me here?

ROSINE. (*Disdainfully*) How considerate you are!
Why not in my bedroom?

BARTHOLO. Does it upset you? I'm sorry, my child.
You're going to finish your lesson, and I don't want to
miss a moment of the pleasure of hearing you.

FIGARO. (*Aside to the* COUNT) We'll never get him

out of here. (*Aloud*) Come on, Bright-Eyes! Boy! A 410
basin and some water—everything the gentleman
needs.

BARTHOLO. That's right—call them! They're so tired
and upset and put upon by your tricks that they had
to go to bed.

FIGARO. Well then, I'll go and get what we need.
Are the things in your room? (*Aside to the* COUNT)
I'm going to get him away.

BARTHOLO. (*Thinking, as he unfastens his bunch of
keys*) No, no, I'd better go myself. (*Aside to the*
COUNT, *as he goes*) Now keep your eye on them, for 420
heaven's sake.

FIGARO. Oh, what a chance we missed! He was
going to give me the keys. The key to the shutter is
there, isn't it?

ROSINE. It's the newest one.

(BARTHOLO *returns.*)

BARTHOLO. (*Aside*) I don't know what got into me,
to leave that cursed barber here. (*To* FIGARO, *giving
him the keys*) Here. In my dressing room, under the
bureau. But don't touch anything else.

FIGARO. Plague on you! It would serve you right if 430
I did, just for being so suspicious. (*Aside as he goes*)
See how heaven protects the innocent!

BARTHOLO. (*Aside to the* COUNT) That's the villain
who delivered the letter to the Count.

COUNT. He looks like a rascal to me.

BARTHOLO. He won't fool me again.

COUNT. I believe the worst is over, in that regard.

BARTHOLO. All in all, I thought it was wiser to send him to my room than to leave him here with her.

440   COUNT. They couldn't exchange a word without my being a party to it.

ROSINE. It's certainly polite of you gentlemen to whisper together so long. How about my lesson?

(*A crash of breaking dishes is heard offstage.*)

BARTHOLO. (*Shouting*) What's that I hear? That pesky barber must have dropped everything on the stairs—all the best things in my dressing case! (*He runs out.*)

COUNT. We must make the most of the moment that Figaro was clever enough to give us. I implore you, Madame, to speak to me for a moment this evening.

450 Without that, we can't save you from the slavery that's about to close around you.

ROSINE. Oh, Lindor!

COUNT. I can climb up to this shutter. Now, about the letter I received from you this morning. I found that I had to—

BARTHOLO (*Returning with* FIGARO) I wasn't mistaken. Everything is broken, smashed.

FIGARO. See what terrible grief this calamity calls for! You can't see a thing on the stairs. (*He shows a*

460 *key to the* COUNT.) On the way up, I stumbled on a key—

BARTHOLO. You should watch what you're doing! Stumble on a key! There's a clever one!

FIGARO. My word, sir, just try to find one any cleverer.

(BAZILE *enters.*)

ROSINE. (*Frightened, aside*) Don Bazile!

COUNT. (*Aside*) Good heavens!

FIGARO. (*Aside*) The devil himself!

BARTHOLO. (*Going to him*) Ah, Bazile, my friend, you've recovered quickly. Your upset didn't lead to 470 anything serious? To tell the truth, Mister Alonzo frightened me about your condition. You can ask him; I was ready to go to see you, and if he hadn't stopped me—

BAZILE. (*Astonished*) Mister Alonzo?

FIGARO. (*Stamping his foot*) What's this, more delays? Two hours to do one miserable beard! What an inconsiderate customer!

BAZILE. (*Gazing around at them all*) Will you kindly tell me, gentlemen—   480

FIGARO. He can tell you after I'm through.

BAZILE. But at least I must—

COUNT. At least you must be quiet, Bazile. Do you think you can tell the gentleman anything he doesn't already know? I told him that you sent me to give the music lesson in your place.

BAZILE. (*More astonished*) The music lesson! Alonzo!

ROSINE. (*Aside to* BAZILE) Sh! Be quiet!

BAZILE. She too?   490

COUNT. (*Aside to* BARTHOLO) Whisper to him that we have it all arranged.

BARTHOLO. (*Aside to* BAZILE) Don't contradict us, Bazile, by saying he's not your substitute. You'll spoil everything.

BAZILE. Oh, ho!

BARTHOLO. (*Aloud*) To tell the truth, Bazile, I never saw a man so talented as your pupil.

BAZILE. (*Stupefied*) My pupil! (*Whispering*) I
500 came to tell you that the Count has gone.

BARTHOLO. (*Whispering*) I know it. Be quiet.

BAZILE. (*Whispering*) Who told you?

BARTHOLO. (*Whispering*) He did, of course.

COUNT. (*Whispering*) I did, of course. Just listen.

ROSINE. (*Aside to* BAZILE) Is it so hard to keep still?

FIGARO. (*Aside to* BAZILE) Ho, you big hippopotamus! He's deaf!

BAZILE. (*Aside*) Who's being fooled around here?
510 They're all in on the secret.

BARTHOLO. (*Aloud*) Well, Bazile, how about that lawyer?

FIGARO. You have all evening to talk about your lawyer.

BARTHOLO. (*To* BAZILE) Just one thing. Are you satisfied with the lawer?

BAZILE. (*Frightened*) With the lawyer?

COUNT. (*Smiling*) Didn't you see the lawyer?

BAZILE. (*Impatiently*) No, I haven't seen the lawyer.

520 COUNT. (*Aside to* BARTHOLO) You don't want him to explain in front of her. Send him away.

BARTHOLO. (*Aside to the* COUNT) You're right. (*To* BAZILE) What made you ill so suddenly?

BAZILE. (*Angrily*) What are you talking about!

COUNT. (*Quietly slipping a purse in his hands*) Yes.

The gentleman wants to know what you're doing here when you're so sick.

FIGARO. He's as pale as death.

BAZILE. Oh, I understand!

COUNT. Go to bed, my dear Bazile. You're not well, 530 and we're worried about you. Go to bed.

FIGARO. He looks all upset. Go to bed.

BARTHOLO. Upon my word, you can feel the fever a mile away! Go to bed!

ROSINE. Why did you ever come out? They say it's catching. Go to bed.

BAZILE. (*Utterly astonished*) I should go to bed?

ALL. Yes, by all means.

BAZILE. (*Looking around at them*) As a matter of fact, I believe it would be a good idea to go to bed. 540 I'm certainly not in my usual state of equilibrium.

BARTHOLO. Come again tomorrow, if you feel better.

COUNT. Bazile, I'll be at your house the first thing in the morning.

FIGARO. Believe me, you'd better keep good and warm in bed.

ROSINE. Goodby, Mister Bazile.

BAZILE. (*Aside*) The devil take me if I know what this is all about. If it weren't for this purse—

ALL. Goodby, Bazile, goodby! 550

BAZILE. (*As he goes*) Well, goodby then, goodby.

(*They watch him go with a burst of laughter.*)

BARTHOLO. (*Pompously*) That man's not at all well.

ROSINE. His eyes are wild.

COUNT. He must have caught a chill.

FIGARO. Did you notice him talking to himself? How frail a creature man is! (*To* BARTHOLO) Now then, are you ready at last? (*He pushes a chair away from the* COUNT *and* ROSINE *and hands a towel to* BARTHOLO.)

COUNT. Before we go on, Madame, I want to tell you something that will help you in the art which I have
560 the honor to teach you. (*He goes near her and whispers in her ear.*)

BARTHOLO. (*To* FIGARO) Hey, there! Are you standing in front of me on purpose, to keep me from seeing?

COUNT. (*Whispering to* ROSINE) We have the key to the shutter, and we'll be here at midnight.

FIGARO. (*Tying the towel around* BARTHOLO's *neck*) Seeing what? If it were a dancing lesson there might be something to see, but a singing lesson—Oh, oh!

BARTHOLO. What's the matter?

FIGARO. I don't know what this is in my eye. (*He shows it to* BARTHOLO.)

BARTHOLO. Don't rub it.

570 FIGARO. It's the left. Will you be good enough to blow on it a little harder?

(BARTHOLO *takes hold of* FIGARO's *head, looks over it, then pushes him aside and goes behind the lovers to listen to their conversation.*)

COUNT. (*Whispering to* ROSINE) And as for your letter, when I couldn't find any other excuse for staying here—

FIGARO. (*Warning them from a distance*) Ahem, ahem!

COUNT. —and in despair at finding my disguise was useless—

BARTHOLO. (*Stepping between them*) Your disguise useless! 580

ROSINE. (*Frightened*) Oh!

BARTHOLO. Very good, Madame. Don't be upset. What's this? Right under my nose, in my presence, you dare an outrage like this!

COUNT. What's the matter with you, sir?

BARTHOLO. You sly fox, Alonzo!

COUNT. Mister Bartholo, if you are often subject to such whims as the one I have just happened to witness, I scarcely wonder that Madame is unwilling to become your wife. 590

ROSINE. Me his wife? Passing my days in the company of a jealous old man who offers my youth no happiness but an abominable slavery!

BARTHOLO. Oh, what's that you're saying?

ROSINE. Yes, I'll say it out loud. I'll give my hand and my heart to any man who can rescue me from this horrible prison, where my person and my property are held unjustly. (*She goes out.*)

BARTHOLO. I'm choking with anger.

COUNT. You see, sir, a young lady finds it hard— 600

FIGARO. Yes, youth coupled with age—that's what troubles an old man's mind.

BARTHOLO. What! When I caught them red-handed? You infernal barber, I'd like to—

FIGARO. I'm getting out of here. He's out of his mind.

COUNT. I'm going too. He must be out of his mind.

FIGARO. Out of his mind! Out of his mind!

(*They go.*)

BARTHOLO. (*Running after them*) Out of my mind!
You infamous cheats! Emissaries of the devil, whose
610 work you carry on here, and may he carry you all off!
I'm out of my mind! Why, I saw them as clearly as I
see this desk—and to brazen it out like that in front
of me! Bazile is the only one who can explain all this.
Yes, I'd better send somebody for him. Hey there,
someone! Oh, I forgot; there isn't anyone to send. A
neighbor, a passer-by—I don't care who. It's enough
to make me lose my wits. It's enough to make me lose
my wits.

(*During the entr'acte the stage is darkened. The orchestra plays music representing the sound of a storm.*)

Act IV

(*The stage is dark. Enter* BARTHOLO *and* DON BAZILE *with a paper lantern in his hand.*)

BARTHOLO. What's that, Bazile? You don't know him? Is that possible?

BAZILE. If you ask me a hundred times, I'll tell you the same. If he gave you Rosine's letter, he must be one of the Count's men. But judging by the munificence of the present he gave me, he might even be the Count himself.

BARTHOLO. Not much chance of that. But speaking of that present, hm? Why did you take it?

BAZILE. You all seemed to be in agreement. I didn't 10 understand any of it. And when a case is hard to decide, a purse of gold always appears to me to be an unanswerable argument. As the proverb says, what's worth taking—

BARTHOLO. I know—is worth returning.

BAZILE. No, no—is worth keeping.

BARTHOLO. (*Surprised*) Oh?

BAZILE. Yes, I have my own versions of a number of these proverbs. But let's come to the point. What are you going to do?   20

BARTHOLO. In my place, Bazile, wouldn't you try every way to hold onto her?

BAZILE. By no means, doctor. When it comes to property, getting hold of it means very little. It's the enjoyment of it that makes us happy. In my opinion, to marry a woman who doesn't love you is to lay yourself open to—

BARTHOLO. You'd be afraid of something going wrong?

30 BAZILE. Ho, ho, sir! There are plenty of examples just this year. I wouldn't try to force her heart.

BARTHOLO. Pardon me, Bazile. I would rather she should weep to have me than that I should die of not having her.

BAZILE. It's a matter of life and death? Then marry her, doctor, marry her.

BARTHOLO. I'll do that, this very night.

BAZILE. Goodby then. Remember when you speak to your ward to paint them blacker than hell.

40 BARTHOLO. You're right.

BAZILE. Slander, doctor, slander. You can't get anywhere without it.

BARTHOLO. Here's Rosine's letter that Alonzo brought me. Without meaning to, he showed me how I can use it to bring her around.

BAZILE. Goodby. We'll all be here at four o'clock.

BARTHOLO. Why not earlier?

BAZILE. That's impossible. The notary has an engagement.

50 BARTHOLO. For a wedding?

BAZILE. Yes, at the barber Figaro's house. His niece is being married.

BARTHOLO. His niece? He hasn't one.

BAZILE. That's what they said at the notary's.

BARTHOLO. That clown must be in on the plot. What the devil!

BAZILE. Would you think—?

BARTHOLO. My word, these fellows are so quick! Look, my friend, I'm worried. Go back to the notary and get him to come here with you immediately. 60

BAZILE. It's raining; the weather is terrible. But nothing stops me from helping you. Where are you going?

BARTHOLO. I'm going to show you out. They got that Figaro to cripple all my servants, and I'm alone here.

BAZILE. I have my lantern.

BARTHOLO. Here, Bazile, here's my passkey. I'll wait up for you; I'll keep watch. And come what may, no one but you and the notary are coming in here tonight.

BAZILE. With these precautions, you're sure to win 70 your case.

(They go out. ROSINE enters from her room.)

ROSINE. I thought I heard someone talking. It's just midnight; Lindor hasn't come. This bad weather is the best thing that could happen; he's sure not to meet a soul. Oh, Lindor, if you're deceiving me— What's that noise? Heavens, it's my guardian! I'd better go back to my room.

BARTHOLO. *(Entering, holding a light)* Oh, Rosine, since you haven't gone to your room yet—

ROSINE. I'm going to retire now.

BARTHOLO. You can't rest in this terrible storm, and 80 I have several important things to say to you.

ROSINE. What do you want, sir? Isn't it enough to be tormented all day?

BARTHOLO. Rosine, listen to me.

ROSINE. I'll listen to you tomorrow.

BARTHOLO. Just a moment, please.

ROSINE. (*Aside*) What if he should come now?

BARTHOLO. (*Showing her the letter*) Do you recognize this letter?

90 ROSINE. (*Recognizing it*) Oh, good heavens!

BARTHOLO. Rosine, I have no intention of reproaching you. A girl makes mistakes at your age. But I'm your friend. Listen to me.

ROSINE. I'm overwhelmed.

BARTHOLO. This letter that you wrote to Count Almaviva—

ROSINE. (*Astonished*) To Count Almaviva?

BARTHOLO. Just look what a dreadful fellow this Count is. As soon as he received it, he showed it off 100 like a trophy. I got it from a woman he gave it to.

ROSINE. Count Almaviva!

BARTHOLO. It's hard for you to believe that he's such a monster. Rosine, inexperience makes your sex confiding and credulous. Let me tell you what a trap you would have fallen into. That woman told me everything; I suppose she wants to get rid of you as a rival. I shudder to think of it! The most abominable conspiracy between Almaviva, Figaro, and Alonzo. That young man pretends to be Bazile's pupil, but his real 110 name is something else, and he's a vile agent of the Count. They almost dragged you into an abyss from which you could never be rescued.

ROSINE. (*Overcome*) How horrible! What, Lindor? What, that young man—?

BARTHOLO. (*Aside*) Oh, so it's Lindor!

ROSINE. And it was for Count Almaviva, it was for another man—

BARTHOLO. That's what I was told when I was given your letter.

ROSINE. (*Outraged*) Oh, what a disgrace! He's going to be punished! Sir, would you like to marry me? 120

BARTHOLO. You know the depth of my feelings.

ROSINE. If you can still feel that way about me, I'm yours.

BARTHOLO. Well, then, the notary will be here this very night.

ROSINE. That's not all. Oh, heavens! My humiliation is even worse. That traitor will soon come in here through that shutter. He was clever enough to steal the key from you. 130

BARTHOLO. (*Looking at his keys*) Oh, those villains! My child, I'll never leave you again.

ROSINE. (*In terror*) Oh, sir, but what if they're armed?

BARTHOLO. You're right; they might escape my revenge. Go up to Marceline's room. Turn the lock twice from the inside. I'm going to call the police and then wait for that fellow near the house. When he's arrested for burglary, we'll have the pleasure of being revenged on him and saved from him at the same time. And remember that my love will repay you— 140

ROSINE. (*In despair*) Only forgive my mistake. (*Aside*) Oh, I'm punished enough for it.

BARTHOLO. (*As he goes off*) I'll go and get ready for him. At last I have her.

ROSINE. His love will repay me! Oh, how unhappy I am! (*She takes out a handkerchief and gives way to tears.*) What shall I do when he comes? I'll stay here and lead him on, so that I can see him for a moment in 150 all his blackness. The evil he has done will save me from him. Oh, and I need something to save me! His noble figure, his lovely manner, his sweet voice! And he's only the vile agent of a seducer! Oh, I'm so unhappy! So unhappy! Heavens! Somebody's opening the shutter!

(*She runs out.* FIGARO, *wrapped in a mantle, appears at the window.*)

FIGARO. (*Speaking to the* COUNT *outside*) Someone just ran out. Shall I go in?

COUNT. (*From outside*) A man?

FIGARO. No.

160 COUNT. It was Rosine. She was frightened away by your ugliness.

FIGARO (*Jumping into the room*) My word, you must be right. Here we are at last, in spite of rain, thunder, and lightning.

(*The* COUNT *appears in the window, also wrapped in a mantle.*)

COUNT. Give me your hand. (*He jumps into the room.*) We've won.

FIGARO. (*Throwing off his mantle*) We're soaked. A

lovely night to go romancing. Sir, how do you like this evening?

COUNT. Perfect for a lover.   170

FIGARO. Yes, but how about the confidant? And suppose someone catches us here?

COUNT. Aren't you with me? I have other things to worry about: how to persuade her to leave her guardian's house tonight.

FIGARO. You have three passions on your side that are very powerful with the fair sex: love, hate, and fear.

COUNT. (*Gazing out into the darkness*) How can I come right out and tell her that the notary is waiting   180 at your house to marry us? She'll think I'm pretty bold. She'll call me audacious.

FIGARO. If she calls you audacious, you call her cruel. Women are utterly delighted when they're called cruel. Besides, if she already loves you for yourself, you can tell her who you are. Then she will no longer doubt your feelings.

(ROSINE *enters.* FIGARO *lights all the candles on the table.*)

COUNT. There she is, my beautiful Rosine!

ROSINE. (*In her calmest tone*) I began to fear, sir,   190 that you weren't coming.

COUNT. How sweet of you to worry! Lady, I don't wish to take advantage of the circumstances to ask you to share the lot of a poor man; but whatever refuge you wish to choose, I swear on my honor—

ROSINE. Sir, if it weren't necessary that the gift of

my hand must immediately follow that of my heart, you wouldn't be here. Let that necessity justify to you whatever irregularity there may be in this interview.

COUNT. Rosine, can such a woman as you share the
200 life of an unfortunate man, without means or position?

ROSINE. Position! Means! Let's disregard everything that depends altogether on mere chance. If you assure me that your intentions are honorable—

COUNT. (*At her feet*) Oh, Rosine, I adore you!

ROSINE. (*Indignantly*) Stop, you wretch! You dare to profane that word! You adore me! Go! You're no danger to me any more. I needed only to hear that word from you in order to detest you. But before I leave you to suffer the remorse that's coming to you—
210 (*Weeping*)—I want you to know that I did love you; I was happy at the thought of sharing your poor life. You wretch, Lindor! I was ready to give up everything to go with you. But the cowardly way you abused my kindness, and the baseness of that horrible Count Almaviva that you sold me to, have put in my hands this evidence of my folly. Do you know this letter?

COUNT. (*Eagerly*) Did your guardian give it to you?

ROSINE (*Proudly*) Yes, I'm indebted to him for it.

COUNT. Good heavens, how happy I am! He got it
220 from me. When I was in a tight spot with him yesterday, I used it to secure his confidence, and I couldn't find a minute to tell you about it. Oh, Rosine! Then it's true that you really love me!

FIGARO. Milord, you wanted a woman who loves you only for yourself.

ROSINE. Milord! What does he mean?

COUNT. (*Throwing off his mantle and appearing magnificently dressed*) Oh, most beloved of women! I can't deceive you any longer. The happy man here at your feet is not Lindor; I am the Count Almaviva, and I nearly died of love while I sought you in vain for six months.

ROSINE. (*Falling into the* COUNT'S *arms*) Oh!

COUNT. (*Frightened*) Figaro?

FIGARO. Don't worry, sir. The sweet emotion of joy has no serious consequences. There now, there now; she's coming around. My word, how beautiful she is!

ROSINE. Oh, Lindor! Oh, sir! How foolish I am. I agreed to marry my guardian this very night!

COUNT. You did, Rosine?

ROSINE. How I would be punished if I had to go through my entire life detesting you! Oh, Lindor, is there anything worse than hate when you want to love?

FIGARO. (*Looking out the window*) Our escape is cut off, sir! The ladder is gone!

COUNT. Gone!

ROSINE. (*Upset*) Yes, it's my fault—the doctor did it. That's the result of my foolishness. He deceived me, and I confessed everything—I betrayed you. He knows you're here, and he's coming with the police.

FIGARO. (*Still looking out*) Someone is coming in, sir.

ROSINE. (*Running in fright into the* COUNT'S *arms*) Oh, Lindor!

COUNT. (*With firm decision*) Rosine, you love me. I'm not afraid of anyone, and you're going to be my wife. I'm going to have the pleasure of punishing the odious old man in my own way.

ROSINE. No, no, forgive him, Lindor. My heart is so full that there's no room in it for vengeance.

(DON BAZILE *enters with the* NOTARY.)

260   FIGARO. It's our notary, sir.

COUNT. And friend Bazile with him.

BAZILE. Oh! What do I see?

FIGARO. Well, how does it happen, my friend—

BAZILE. How does it happen, gentlemen—

NOTARY. Is this the happy couple?

COUNT. Yes, sir. You were going to marry Señora Rosine and me tonight at the barber Figaro's house. But we have certain reasons for preferring this house. Do you have our contract?

270   NOTARY. Then I have the honor to speak to His Excellency Count Almaviva?

FIGARO. Precisely.

BAZILE. (*Aside*) If this is what he gave me the pass-key for—

NOTARY. Now, I have two marriage contracts here. We must not confuse them. Here is yours, and here is Doctor Bartholo's, with Señora—Rosine also? No doubt the two ladies are sisters, with the same name?

COUNT. Let's sign right away. Don Bazile will serve

280 as the second witness.

(*They sign.*)

BAZILE. But, Your Excellency—I don't understand—

COUNT. Mister Bazile, the merest trifle is enough to

confuse you, and you're astonished by everything.

BAZILE. But, sir—if the doctor—

COUNT. (*Throwing him a purse.*) You're acting like a child. Go ahead and sign.

BAZILE. (*Astonished*) Oh, oh!

FIGARO. What's so difficult about signing?

BAZILE. (*Weighing the purse*) No difficulty any longer. But when I've once given my word, I must 290 have reasons of the greatest weight—

(*He signs.* BARTHOLO *enters with the* ALCALDE, *policemen, and servants with torches. He finds the* COUNT *kissing* ROSINE's *hand, and* FIGARO *grotesquely embracing* DON BAZILE. *He cries out and seizes the* NOTARY *by the throat.*)

BARTHOLO. Rosine with these villains! Arrest everybody! I have one of them by the collar.

NOTARY. I'm your notary.

BAZILE. He's your notary. Are you fooling?

BARTHOLO. Oh, Don Bazile, eh? What are you doing here?

BAZILE. That's not the question. Why weren't you here?

ALCALDE. (*Pointing to* FIGARO) Just a minute. I 300 know this fellow. What are you doing in this house at this time of night?

FIGARO. What do you mean, this time of night? You can see it's as near morning as evening. Besides, I'm in the service of His Excellency Count Almaviva.

BARTHOLO. Almaviva!

ALCALDE. Then they aren't thieves?

BARTHOLO. Let's forget about that. Everywhere else, Count, I'm at Your Excellency's service; but you
310 understand that superiority in rank means nothing here. If you please, be good enough to leave.

COUNT. It's true that rank counts for nothing here. But what counts a great deal is the preference the young lady has shown for me over you, by voluntarily giving herself to me.

BARTHOLO. What's he saying, Rosine?

ROSINE. It's true. Why are you so astonished? Didn't I plan to be avenged on a deceiver this very night? Well, I am.

320 BAZILE. I told you it was the Count himself, doctor.

BARTHOLO. What difference does that make! It's no kind of marriage. Where are the witnesses?

NOTARY. Everything is in order. These two men assisted us.

BARTHOLO. What's that? Bazile, you signed it?

BAZILE. How could I help it? This devil of a man always has his pockets full of irresistible arguments.

BARTHOLO. I have no use for arguments. I'll use my authority.

330 COUNT. You lost it by abusing it.

BARTHOLO. The young lady is a minor.

FIGARO. She just came of age, by marrying.

BARTHOLO. Who asked you, you rascal?

COUNT. The young lady is noble and beautiful. I am a man of rank, young and rich. She is my wife. Does anyone wish to dispute this situation, which is honorable for both of us?

BARTHOLO. Nobody's going to take her out of my hands.

COUNT. You no longer have any power over her. I put her under the protection of the law. This gentleman, whom you brought here yourself, will protect her from any violence you may try to offer her. A just magistrate is the guardian of anyone who is oppressed.

ALCALDE. Certainly. These useless objections to an honorable marriage lead me to think that he's afraid we'll discover some mismanagement of his ward's property. He must render a complete account of it.

COUNT. Oh, if he'll consent to our marriage, I won't ask him for any of it.

FIGARO. Except a quittance for my hundred écus. Let's not lose our heads.

BARTHOLO. (*Annoyed*) They're all against me. I've pushed my head into a hornet's nest.

BAZILE. It's no hornet's nest. When you give up the lady, remember the money stays with you, doctor, with you.

BARTHOLO. Oh, leave me alone, Bazile. You think of nothing but money. What do I care about money? Of course I'll keep it, but that's not why I give my consent. (*He signs.*)

FIGARO. (*Laughing*) Ha, ha, ha! They belong to the same family, sir!

NOTARY. But, gentlemen, I don't quite understand. Aren't there two ladies with the same name?

FIGARO. No, sir, there's only one.

BARTHOLO. (*Disconsolate*) And I am the one who

carried off the ladder to make their marriage certain. I lost for lack of care.

370   FIGARO. Lack of sense. But to tell the truth, doctor, when youth and love conspire together to deceive an old man, anything he might do to stop them may well be called *The Useless Precaution*.

BIBLIOGRAPHY

ON BEAUMARCHAIS

Cox, Cynthia, *The Real Figaro, the Extraordinary Career of Caron de Beaumarchais.* (New York, 1963).

Dalsème, René, *Beaumarchais,* trans. by Hannaford Bennett. (New York, 1929).

Frischauer, Paul, *Beaumarchais, Adventurer in the Century of Women,* trans. by Margaret Goldsmith. (New York, 1935).

Lemaitre, Georges, *Beaumarchais.* (New York, 1949).

Rivers, John, *Figaro, the Life of Beaumarchais.* (London, 1922).

ON THE THEATER OF THE TIME

Duchartre, Pierre Louis, *The Italian Comedy,* trans. by Randolph T. Weaver. (London, 1929).

Lough, John, *Paris Theatre Audiences in the Seventeenth and Eighteenth Centuries.* (London, 1957).